THE
ACCUSATION

THE
ACCUSATION

BLOOD LIBEL
in an American Town

EDWARD BERENSON

W. W. NORTON & COMPANY
Independent Publishers Since 1923

For information about permission to reproduce selections from this book, write to
Permissions, W. W. Norton & Company, Inc., 500 Fifth Avenue, New York, NY 10110

For information about special discounts for bulk purchases, please contact
W. W. Norton Special Sales at specialsales@wwnorton.com or 800-233-4830

Manufacturing by Worzalla
Book design by JAM Design
Production manager: Julia Druskin

Library of Congress Cataloging-in-Publication Data

Names: Berenson, Edward, 1949– author.
Title: The accusation : blood libel in an American town / Edward Berenson.
Description: New York ; London : W. W. Norton & Company, independent
publishers since 1923, [2019] | Includes bibliographical references and index.
Identifiers: LCCN 2019020009 | ISBN 9780393249422 (hardcover)
Subjects: LCSH: Blood accusation—New York (State)—Massena—History—20th
Century. | Jews—New York (State)—Massena—History. | Massena (N.Y.)—
Ethnic relations. | Antisemitism—United States—History—20th Century.
Classification: LCC BM585.2 .B47 2019 | DDC 305.892/4074756—dc23
LC record available at https://lccn.loc.gov/2019020009

W. W. Norton & Company, Inc., 500 Fifth Avenue, New York, N.Y. 10110
www.wwnorton.com

W. W. Norton & Company Ltd., 15 Carlisle Street, London W1D 3BS

1 2 3 4 5 6 7 8 9 0

In memory of my father,
Norman Berenson
(1919–2018)

Contents

THE
ACCUSATION

Prologue

A CHILD DISAPPEARS

O n Saturday, September 22, 1928, four-year-old Barbara
Griffiths strayed into the woods surrounding Massena,
New York, an upstate village overlooking the broad St.
Lawrence River. Barbara's mother had sent her to look for her
older brother Bobby, who was playing with friends. At 6 P.M.,
Bobby came home for dinner, as he always did, but without his
sister in tow. Alarmed, the children's father, Dave, told Bobby
and his gang to fan out around the town while he headed into
the woods. When Dave failed to locate his daughter, he alerted
the Massena police, whose chief sounded the fire horn to sum-
mon the town's volunteer firefighters to the Griffiths' house.
From there, the uniformed men organized a massive search
for the missing girl. By 7 P.M., some 300 people were combing
through dozens of homes and ranging deep into the forest. The
hunt for the missing child continued through the night and into

Barbara Griffiths, age four

the following day. To no avail. By midafternoon on Sunday, Barbara still had not been found.[1]

Her parents were frantic and the townspeople on edge. Everyone knew Barbara, who was an adorable post-toddler and wise beyond her years. A picture taken shortly before Barbara's disappearance shows her with page-boy hair and a pensive smile. She stands at a right angle to the camera, but her head, slightly bowed, faces the photographer boldly. She's neatly, but not fancily, dressed, with loose leggings, a dress floating just above her knees, and a short double-breasted coat. Most adults would have found her precious, which is why so many had jumped so readily into the effort to find her.

Had Barbara fallen and hit her head? Had she been attacked by animals? Indians? An escaped criminal? Or had something more diabolical taken place?

Several hours into the search, someone—it's unclear who— floated the idea that Barbara had been kidnapped and killed by the Jews. She was the victim, voices said, of ritual murder, of the Jews' supposed need to ritually kill Christian children and harvest their blood. The legend of ritual murder, one of the ugliest and most persistent features of the antisemitic imagination, first emerged in medieval England. It held that Jews required young Christian blood for matzo-making or other darkly religious needs. Corporal H. M. (Mickey) McCann, the state police officer called in to direct the search for Barbara, said the ritual murder accusation originated with a "foreigner" living in town and that he believed it.[2] So did Massena's mayor, W. Gilbert Hawes.[3] Beyond these accounts, other reports maintained that local firefighters belonging to the Ku Klux Klan, much revived in the 1920s, had launched the ritual murder accusation, and still others claimed that the foreigner in question was one of the many French Canadians employed at Massena's huge Alcoa Aluminum plant.[4]

In any case, the accusation of ritual murder suddenly took hold. The mayor, state police officers, and hundreds of villagers discarded every other scenario except the notion that the Jews had killed Barbara Griffiths, surely the least plausible of all the explanations villagers had advanced. That so many jumped to this conclusion was especially bizarre because this accusation against Jews, although common in Europe, was essentially unknown in the United States. A few reports of isolated accusations with little community response appeared from time to time in Yiddish-language newspapers, but Massena stands as the unique case of the "blood libel," as the Jews called it, gripping an entire American town and taken seriously by the authorities.[5]

Why Massena, New York? And why there but nowhere else in the United States—and at no other time? What did the accusation and its outcome say about the place of Jews in American life, especially in the wake of intense, weeks-long press coverage of the incident nationwide? And how, ultimately, did American attitudes about Jews compare with European ones?

These questions, and others, moved me to delve into what would be both a personal family history and the history of the blood libel against the Jews. I was born in Massena, my father's birthplace as well, and my research took me back to the village for the first time in nearly forty years. My great-grandparents, Jesse J. Kauffman and Ida Tarshis Kauffman, were perhaps the first Jewish residents of the village, landing there in 1898 with their two baby girls, Harriet (my grandmother) and Sadie. Their son Abe was the first Jewish child born in the village. Both Jesse and Ida had come to the United States as teenagers in the early years of the massive Jewish influx from Central and Eastern Europe. Their birthplaces had once belonged to Poland, but after the partition of that country in 1815, Jesse's hometown, Bielica, ended up in Prussia and eventually the German Empire, while Ida's, Aran, was integrated into the Russian Empire.[6] Jesse started out in New York City as a delivery boy and, like so many other young Jewish men, soon turned to peddling.[7] He followed the Erie Canal north to Albany, then west to Utica, and finally due north again until he ran into the St. Lawrence River and the Canadian border at Ogdensburg, New York.

As a male, even a young one, Jesse could emigrate by himself. Ida came with her brother and his family, and their trajectory stretched from Boston to Burlington, Vermont, before arriving in Ogdensburg at around the same time as Jesse in the early 1890s. Ida ran a small general store until she married Jesse in 1895. The couple soon decamped to Massena, attracted by business opportunities in a town whose economy seemed about to take off. It had been an agricultural backwater until then.

Massena was the last part of New York State settled by Europeans. After the American Revolution, the U.S. government gained rights to the area by giving the Mohawk Indians a lump sum and the promise of annual payments. This transaction was interpreted differently by the United States and by the American Indians, and ownership of parts of the land remains in dispute to this day. U.S. officials believed the land belonged to the government, and they urged people to move there to prevent the British from pushing the Canadian border to the south. Most of the newcomers hailed from New England and came in search of cheap, arable land, though the climate was rude, with winter temperatures sometimes dropping to −30°F. The St. Lawrence River drew settlers as well, since lumbermen could fell trees

Massena, New York

from the virgin forests and float logs down to Montreal and Quebec, where ships and furniture were built.[8]

The town of Massena itself is far from beautiful, sitting as it does on the flat plain that extends from the St. Lawrence River to the first rises of the Adirondack Mountains. The mountains are stunning, and each season gives them a different kind of beauty, from the glistening snow of the long winter months to the dark waters of the pristine glacial lakes. Just north of Massena, the St. Lawrence River flows lazily toward the town before erupting into the Long Sault rapids. This roaring waterway divides the St. Lawrence into separate channels, long impassible on the north side and navigable downstream only on the south. These rapids would be tamed only with the building of the St. Lawrence Seaway in the late 1950s.

Two tributaries of the St. Lawrence, the Grasse and

Raquette Rivers, cut through the village of Massena and give it a certain charm. The various bridges that cross the waterways distinguish Massena from other, riverless upstate towns, although spring floods regularly washed the bridges away. These flowing tributaries encouraged the building of sawmills, gristmills, cement mills, and woolen mills, all of which lifted the economy but did little to beautify the town. Still, by the 1920s, Massena's Main Street would boast two rows of solid-looking brick and limestone buildings, many of them housing Jewish shops.

Side streets accommodated dozens of impressive homes. Industrial workers, however, lived in modest quarters. The Alcoa Aluminum plant, built close to the St. Lawrence, marred certain river views, but elsewhere in Massena, the St. Lawrence shimmered majestically to the north. Equally impressive was Barnhart Island, one of the largest of the great river's many slivers of land. Massena annexed the island in 1814, after the close of the British-American War of 1812.

Main Street, Massena, late 1920s

American Indians had lived in or traversed what became Massena for hundreds of years before 1812. The pioneering Europeans who settled in Massena after the American Revolution found themselves isolated from the rest of the United States, perched as they were in an ill-defined borderland on a northern edge of the country. They found themselves hemmed in to the north and west by the St. Lawrence River, which was frozen three to four months of the year, and to the south by the forbidding Adirondack Mountains. The Erie Canal was a rigorous 150 miles to the south, and the sole route east to Vermont depended on a narrow footpath that snaked through thick forests and dead-ended into Lake Champlain.

Massena's early inhabitants likely didn't feel much sense of belonging to the United States; the town was named by French-speaking migrants after the Napoleonic general André Masséna. This was an odd choice perhaps, since his armies committed terrible atrocities in Sicily and elsewhere during the French military campaigns.[9] A nascent U.S. identity took hold during the War of 1812, when the government feared a British invasion from the north and placed the village on alert. But an invasion never came, and a solid U.S. belonging lay decades in the future. The historian Pierre Birnbaum has argued that, in Europe, ritual murder accusations occurred in isolated or liminal places situated beyond the centralizing reach of the nation-state.[10] In the Massena case, this explanation would not suffice.

For most of the nineteenth century, Massena's economy was built around agriculture, mainly for subsistence in the early decades, and for regional markets as roads were built subsequently. The town's first major industry was dairy farming, but entrepreneurs also established several small sawmills powered

by the swift current of the Grasse River. After Massena residents discovered two natural sulfur springs in the 1820s, the village became a small mecca for the nineteenth century's version
of medical tourism. Local Indians had long used the springs
for medicinal purposes, naming them *Kanaswastakeras*, or "the
place where the mud smells bad." And like the Native Americans, doctors of the era commonly believed that "taking the
waters" would cure a variety of ailments, from skin diseases
to ulcers. A few hotels were built to house the spa-goers, but
Massena remained too isolated—even after a railroad went in—
to become a major center for the water cure. In the late nineteenth century, it succumbed to competition from more easily
reached places such as Saratoga Springs, New York, and even
Hot Springs, Arkansas.

What transformed Massena's economy was the building of a
three-mile-long power canal to harness the hydroelectric potential of the St. Lawrence and Grasse Rivers, which run parallel to
each other three to four miles apart before the Grasse empties
into the big river downstream. Since the St. Lawrence sits nearly
fifty feet above the Grasse, engineers realized that by building a
canal that sloped downward from the higher river to the lower
river, they could capture the power of the St. Lawrence's water
as it dropped to the Grasse River below. The project, begun
in August 1897, required 2,000 workers; to find them on the
cheap, the Lehigh Construction Company recruited immigrant
labor right off the ships at Ellis Island. A great many of these
workers were Roman Catholics from Italy, Poland, Ireland, and
Austria-Hungary.

The canal's powerhouse contained what was then the largest
collection of electricity-generating machinery in the world, and

Digging the power canal

it attracted the interest of the Pittsburgh Reduction Company, later known as the Aluminum Company of America, or Alcoa.[11] This firm was the United States's first aluminum processing concern, having set up shop in Pittsburgh in 1888.[12] In search of more power to meet the growing demand for the lightweight, durable metal, the enterprise built a subsidiary in Niagara Falls, New York, in 1895, and then in Massena in 1902. Many alumni of the town's completed power canal project went to work for Alcoa, but the rapidly growing smelting plant needed so many laborers that it also recruited directly from steerage class at Ellis Island and from French and English Canada. The number of workers blossomed from the original 67 to 1,200 in 1914, 2,500 in 1915, and 3,000 in 1920.[13]

My grandfather, Edward Berenson, was one of those Alcoa workers, having earned a degree in chemical engineering at MIT. In 1917, he moved from his hometown of Boston to Massena after being offered the Alcoa job. Ed's wife-to-be, Harriet Kauffman, the daughter of Jesse and Ida, attended a two-year college in Syracuse and found employment as a secretary at the St. Lawrence Power Company, which now oversaw Massena's power canal. Shortly after marrying in 1919, they left their respective jobs to open a store and eventually joined the main family business, Kauffman's Department Store.[14]

With the power canal and then Alcoa, Massena was transformed almost overnight from a largely agricultural community of Protestant, "old-stock" Americans to an industrial boomtown with an ethnically and religious diverse population of Catholics, Protestants, Greek Orthodox, and Jews. In 1870, the village of Massena contained just 483 souls, virtually all white Protestants. The village's population more than doubled to 1,049 in 1890 and doubled again to just over 2,000 in 1900. It rose to 2,951 in 1910, 5,993 in 1920, and 10,637 in 1930.[15] The 1930 United States Census shows that nearly 30 percent of the village's residents (3,091) were foreign-born and that, for another 27 percent, one or both of their parents had been born abroad. Seventy percent of the non–native-born residents had come from Canada, equally divided between French- and English-speaking provinces. Most of the rest had emigrated from Russia and Eastern Europe (11.6 percent), Italy (5.6 percent), and England (3 percent). The makeup of people with foreign or mixed parents was similar.[16] Many of these immigrants had not become U.S. citizens by 1930, with about half of Massena's adult inhabitants still aliens at this time.[17]

The village's meager housing stock couldn't begin to accommodate the influx of immigrants, who were forced at first to live in tarpaper shanties without heat or running water. Most were single men; the married ones had left their wives and children behind. Lacking diversions other than drink from their harsh conditions of work and life, they tussled with one another and with the local St. Regis Indians. More than a few long-standing residents became hostile to these "uncouth" foreigners and lamented their presence in town. The progressives tended to be equally unenthusiastic about the immigrants' alien cultures but took steps to assimilate the newcomers by establishing "Americanization" courses designed to teach them English and instill "American values." Immigrants often resisted such forced Americanization, and ethnic and religious tensions simmered beneath the surface of this rapidly changing town.

Alcoa had sparked this influx of immigrants, and after a few years in business, the company became Massena's largest employer; it would remain so for nearly a century. Alcoa's workforce was male, save for a handful of secretaries and bookkeepers, but new industries—an insulation company, a silk mill, and a lingerie factory—provided jobs for the wives and daughters of Alcoa workers and other women who wanted employment outside their homes. These working people needed housing, food, clothing, and other consumer goods, which stimulated the local economy all the more and attracted other newcomers, especially Jews like my great-grandfather, with experience in retail trade.[18]

By the 1920s, roughly half of Massena's commercial establishments belonged to Jewish families—and, as in other small American towns, virtually all of Massena's Jews owned or operated retail businesses.[19] Several became successful, and their prosperity evoked both resentment and admiration. Massena's Jews tended to perceive the resentment more acutely than the admiration, and the blood libel would hit them hard.[20] The ritual murder accusation, the 102-year-old Alice Rosen told me, convinced Massena's Jews—she was sixteen at the time—that a pogrom was imminent.[21]

Like Rosen, Doris Robinson, age ninety-four at the time of our interview, ended up in Massena because her father had fled anti-Jewish discrimination in Russia. After being cleared through Ellis Island, he saw a sign advertising employment opportunities at Alcoa and immediately boarded a train to Massena, where he became one of only a handful of Jewish workers. Doris also took a job at Alcoa, a "woman's job" as a bookkeeper, and stayed there forty-four years. Doris was too young in 1928 to have many direct memories of the blood libel, but the incident, she said, affected her life. At Alcoa, her boss was none other than Dave Griffiths, the father of the girl who had wandered into the woods, unwittingly creating the affair. Dave regularly asked Doris if she had animosity toward him and other Gentiles in the town, and she said she didn't. But she remembered being called a "Christ-killer" as a child, and whenever a strike broke out at Alcoa, she endured anti-Jewish hostility while walking picket lines. One man told her, "Hitler had the right idea," and several blamed Jews for the labor unrest.

Even so, Massena was too small a town to keep Jews and Gentiles apart, and relations between the two were civil, if not always cordial. There were a few Jew-Gentile romantic attachments in the village, but familial pressures on both sides placed marriage beyond the pale. Doris said that several of Massena's Jewish men and women remained unmarried for life because they were romantically attached to a Gentile. This was true of my great-aunt Sadie Kauffman, who lived alone until she died.

Bennett Abrams, a Jew, and Rita McDonald, a Catholic, had a decades-long, semi-clandestine relationship, both unwilling to marry across the barrier of religion. Tragically, as if in a pulp nineteenth-century novel, they finally made their relationship official as Rita suffered on her deathbed.[22]

In 1928, Massena's twenty Jewish families lived in their own religious world, having created a synagogue from the repurposed Congregational Church in 1919.[23] Until then, the town's devout Jewish men had conducted their own services in an old village lodge. With their first bona-fide synagogue came a full-time rabbi, Berel Brennglass, who had been working in the Adirondack village of Tupper Lake. Brennglass was born in Lithuania and attended a yeshiva there before emigrating to Wales and then New York City. He migrated upstate in search of a cure for his tuberculosis.[24] Like their rabbi, essentially all of Massena's Jews had come from the region of Eastern Europe where what are now Lithuania, Poland, and Belarus come together. They shared the same dialect of Yiddish, the same tastes in food, and the same Orthodox Jewish practices and beliefs. Many were related by blood or marriage.[25] This compact community, its members grateful to be in the United States rather than imperial or Bolshevik Russia, suddenly found themselves transported back to the Old World of anti-Jewish hostility from which they had fled.

Chapter 1

THE ACCUSATION

At some point during the night of September 22, 1928, Corporal Mickey McCann of the state police and Mayor Hawes decided to take seriously the rumor circulating through town that the Jews kidnapped and ritualistically killed Barbara Griffiths for her blood. Although there is no consensus about the source of this rumor—possibilities include a Greek café owner, an unidentified "foreigner," a French Canadian, and firefighters belonging to the Ku Klux Klan—a variety of Massenans agreed that two local Jews unwittingly had something to do with it. One was Willie Shulkin, the twenty-one-year-old son of Jake Shulkin, president of Congregation Adath Israel. For reasons never made clear, McCann resolved to interview Willie late on Saturday night. When asked about Jews and ritual sacrifice, Willie seemed to suggest it might occur, but his comments were so rambling and incoherent that the state trooper decided

he was "of low mentality" and released him to his parents.[1]
Willie was known for behavior problems and trouble in school.
Today he might have a diagnosis—bipolar disorder, perhaps, or
autism spectrum disorder—but back then he was simply considered retarded or strange.

When Willie told his parents he had been questioned about
ritual murder, they became alarmed and quickly warned other
members of the Jewish community that a blood libel might be
brewing. Massena's Jews were intimately familiar with both
the ancient and recent history of this scurrilous and dangerous charge, and they decided to seek help. At about 10 P.M., Jake
Shulkin telephoned Louis Marshall, president of the American
Jewish Committee and perhaps the most visible American Jewish
figure. The conversation lasted for more than an hour, and both
Marshall and Massena's Jewish leaders decided that the ritual
murder accusation threatened the safety, and possibly the lives,
of the upstate town's Jewish families. It was, as Shulkin put it, an
urgent "national affair," which required Marshall's intervention.[2]
The Jewish leader dispatched the journalist Boris Smolar of the
Jewish Telegraphic Agency to Massena to cover the story.

Meanwhile, Dave Griffiths, along with police officers and firefighters, friends, neighbors, and some 300 other members of the
community, continued the hunt for Barbara. In a town of 10,000
inhabitants, this was a large search party. David and Marion
Griffiths, both thirty-nine at the time of Barbara's disappearance,
were popular, respected members of the Massena community.
They were active in the Emmanuel Congregational Church, and
Dave, having served in the First World War, was a charter member of Massena's American Legion Post No. 79. He also belonged
to the Beta Phi Pi fraternity and the Hedgehog Sporting Club.

Marion led the Massena Garden Club, winning prizes for her flower arrangements, and sang in her church choir.[3]

Both had come to Massena as adults, Dave from nearby Richville, New York, Marion from Derry, New Hampshire. They met at the Pinkerton Academy, a boarding school in southern New Hampshire, but didn't marry until nearly fifteen years after graduation. Dave had earlier been engaged to Marion's sister, who wed another man while he was fighting overseas. Dave earned a degree in accounting at St. Lawrence University, while Marion studied elementary education at the Salem State Normal School and taught afterwards in Beverly, Massachusetts.

At the time of their marriage in November 1921, Dave took a job as a theater manager after being laid off from Alcoa, where he had worked before and after the war. Marion left her full-time teaching position but taught Sunday school at her church and substituted in the Massena schools. The couple's first child was born in 1923 and Barbara fourteen months later. Dave returned to Alcoa in 1926 and remained there for more than three decades. He started as a shipping clerk and rose to head shipping clerk after twenty-one years on the job.[4] Pictures of Dave taken in 1926 show a good-looking man with dark hair and a warm smile. In photographs taken earlier, Marion appears attractive, if not beautiful, with a svelte figure, dark brown hair parted on the side, and bright oval eyes. She seems shy in front of the camera, rarely venturing a smile.[5]

The Griffiths seemed to know everyone in town, and as night settled in, scores of new people joined the search for their daughter. Many came from the Congregational Church, which Marion attended every Sunday without fail, and from Dave's hunting club, which boasted dozens of men.[6] Temperatures

Dave Griffiths with his aunt, 1926

Marion Blood in 1912

were dropping rapidly in what was already autumn in this northern town, and Dave and Marion's apprehension grew. Friends urged them to wait at home, while they sent a growing number of people into the woods to hunt for Barbara. But Dave was too worried to sit still. Armed with flashlights and lanterns, he and the other searchers pushed deep into the forest, repeatedly calling Barbara's name. They later told journalists, "every foot of ground in the woods and elsewhere in the vicinity had been so thoroughly searched that there could be no possibility of overlooking the child."[7]

Coming up empty-handed in the woods, the search parties returned to the village, where some thought Barbara's body might be found. According to several reports, certain firemen shone their flashlights into the town's closed-up Jewish shops and peered through basement windows to see if the body had been hidden below. Finding nothing, the men returned to the fields and woods surrounding the town. When dawn broke, Barbara still had not turned up. The searchers now mobilized a fleet of cars and trucks, driving into every country lane and stopping regularly to tromp through the brush. Still no Barbara.[8]

The rumors of ritual murder that had surfaced during the night now circulated from one end of the village to the other. Mayor Hawes and Corporal McCann threw themselves into what they now believed might be a murder investigation. (Massena's police chief, Floyd SanJule, withdrew from the case because the search for Barbara took place outside the village limits and beyond his jurisdiction.)

W. Gilbert Hawes, mayor of Massena, 1922–31

Hawes was a prosperous dairy farmer who had married well and become a wealthy man. He owned one of the oldest and grandest homes in the village, the John B. Andrews House, which presided over two and a half acres of land near the center of town. The 1930 census lists the value of Hawes's property at $30,000, five times the national median home value that year, and Massena's prices ranked considerably below the national level.[9] Hawes prided himself on his standing in the community, leading several of Massena's civic, economic, and religious organizations. By 1928, he had been elected mayor seven consecutive times in Massena's annual contests and enjoyed the support of both the Republican and Democratic Parties, thanks to his apparent competence as a local administrator. When Hawes first became mayor in March 1922, Massena possessed not a single paved street; seven years later, the downtown was covered with asphalt and sidewalks and curbs had been installed. The village grew quickly during those years, permitting Hawes to reduce per capita taxation while improving Massena's water system, sewage treatment, and sanitation.[10]

Much less is known about the state police trooper, H. M. (Mickey) McCann, assigned to Massena in 1928. McCann, a veteran of the First World War, was thirty years old, unmarried, and living alone in nearby Gouverneur, where he belonged to the Elks Club and the American Legion. He joined the state police in 1925 after working in a variety of manufacturing jobs.[11]

Early on Sunday, September 23, McCann interviewed a thirty-year-old Alcoa worker named Morris Goldberg; it's unclear why, except for his overtly Jewish name. Goldberg lived on the margins of Massena's Jewish community, having been raised in a Catholic orphanage and the lone Massena Jew married to a Gentile.[12] When asked whether Jews committed ritual murder, Goldberg, "knowing nothing of Judaism, pleaded ignorance, but the clumsy way in which he phrased his answer somehow left a hint that there might be something in the ritual murder charge after all."[13] European ritual murder cases often gained strength from renegade or outcast Jews or from those with intellectual disabilities.[14]

Having spoken with Shulkin and Goldberg, McCann consulted Hawes, and the two resolved to continue their inquiry into ritual murder. They then took the fateful step of summoning Rabbi Brennglass to the town hall, a solid limestone building in the heart of the village. The two officials wanted to question him about Jews and human sacrifice. To get to the hall, the rabbi had to wade through a crowd of some 300 to 400 people amassed outside. There are conflicting reports about the temper of the crowd. Some depicted it as hostile and menacing; others found it calm but watchful, with someone shouting, "Here comes the Rabbi at last."[15] There is no official transcript of the interrogation, but Brennglass recorded it immediately afterwards, and the two officials didn't dispute his version of what happened.

I was asked by the trooper the following questions: Do you know that a child was lost? I answered yes. Have you a holiday tomorrow? Answer, Yes. Could you inform me if your people in the old country are offering human sacrifices on a holiday? Answer: I am dreadfully surprised to hear such a foolish, ridiculous and contemptible question from an officer in the United States of America, which is the most enlightened and civilized country in the world. Do you realize the seriousness of this question? The trooper said then that a foreigner told him so. I told him that it is a false and malicious accusation.[16]

The rabbi added that when asked if the Jewish people ever use human blood, he replied that Jewish law forbids the use of human, or even animal, blood for any purpose. Ashamed, perhaps, McCann repeated that the accusation against the Jews of Massena hadn't originated with him but rather from a foreigner, by which he doubtless meant a relatively recent immigrant to the United States.[17]

Rabbi Berel Brennglass

After the meeting, Brennglass had to push once again through the crowd of people in a "state of excitement," as he put it. The rabbi walked the short distance to his synagogue, where members of the congregation had gathered for the afternoon prayer service on the eve of Yom Kippur, the Day of Atonement, the holiest holiday on the Jewish calendar. Most had heard about the rumors of ritual murder sluicing through the town, and the rabbi's interrogation by McCann and Hawes hardly allayed their mounting fears. What would happen if Barbara could not be found? Or worse, what if her dead body were discovered in the woods? Coming from Eastern Europe, the heartland of the blood libel in the late nineteenth and early twentieth centuries, the Jews of Massena began to fear the worst. Would the Jews, collectively, be accused of murder? Would there be a pogrom? Would the Klan organize a lynching with the complicity of Massena's public officials?

But wasn't America different from Europe—more tolerant, more enlightened, more civilized, as the rabbi had told his interrogators? Still, the ritual murder accusation had surfaced amid an extraordinarily divisive 1928 presidential election, a campaign dripping with religious prejudice, albeit against the Catholicism of the Democratic candidate, New York governor Al Smith. Some of this religious hostility spilled over onto America's Jews, who had already endured Henry Ford's decade-long, rhetorically violent campaign against them, a campaign that featured the notorious antisemitic forgery, *The Protocols of the Elders of Zion*.[18]

More anti-Jewish venom had come from the Ku Klux Klan, which resurfaced during the First World War and peaked at perhaps four million members in 1924.[19] Klan membership shrank dramatically in the second half of the 1920s, but the election of 1928 revived its fortunes, as it joined the broad opposition to Catholicism and the effort to preserve Prohibition, which Smith disliked. The KKK established a significant presence in Massena and burned crosses there during the presidential campaign.[20] Finally, Montreal, just 80 miles away, had seen a powerful wave of antisemitic agitation during the 1920s, and the ritual murder accusation figured prominently in the denunciations of the Jews—as it had in Quebec City a decade earlier.[21]

What exactly was the blood libel and where did it come from? Historians generally agree that the first significant accusation that Jews practiced ritual murder surfaced in England in the mid-twelfth century. The author of this accusation was an English monk named Thomas of Monmouth, whose two-volume treatise, *The Life and Passion of Saint William the Martyr of Norwich*, claimed that in 1144, the Jews of Norwich "bought a Christian child [William] before Easter and tortured him with all the torture that our Lord was tortured with; and on Good Friday hanged him on a cross."[22] Thomas says he heard this story "from the lips" of Theobald, a disillusioned Jew who had converted to Christianity and become a monk. Theobald's story of William's supposed murder was credible, Thomas wrote, because it came from "a converted enemy [who] had been privy to the secrets of our enemies [the Jews]."[23]

It seems clear that Theobald detested his former religious community and invented a series of terrible stories about them. The most important story for Thomas's purposes was that the Jews ritually slaughtered one Christian every year, each time in

William of Norwich, fifteenth century. Artist unknown

a different place. In 1144, Norwich had been selected. The only problem for Thomas's narrative was that Theobald had been nowhere near Norwich that year and could not have witnessed the supposed ritual murder. Either Theobald made up his tale or Thomas created a fictional character named Theobald. Historians think Theobald was real, so it was he, rather than Thomas, who devised the false story of the Jews' ritual murder. Thomas seems to have added the notion that William was crucified, turning him into a Christ-like martyr and eventually a saint.

Neither Thomas nor Theobald said anything about the Jewish consumption of human blood.

A significant number of Thomas's contemporaries were justly skeptical of his tale of Jewish ritual murder, and he responded by publishing a second volume of his work. That volume contains so many contradictions and implausible assertions, not to mention exculpatory evidence about William's death, that it undermines itself and allows us to see just how thin Thomas's accusation was. Only in volume two do we learn, for example, that many residents of Norwich rejected the notion that the Jews had murdered William and that nothing beyond the say-so of a single biased family and Theobald's questionable testimony connected Jews to the crime. Thomas goes so far as to quote critics who were "utterly uncertain as to who killed him [William] and why and how"—only, of course, to dismiss them. In Thomas's own telling, it thus seems highly unlikely that the Jews could have been responsible for having murdered William, let alone tortured and crucified him.[24]

Around 1150, however, travelers to Norwich began to experience miraculous cures, and partly with Thomas's help, they decided that William's supposed martyrdom must have been the cause. Pilgrims now flocked to Norwich, and they circulated the story of William's crucifixion at Jewish hands. By 1170, the tale of the supposed Norwich ritual murder had crossed over to France, where two young boys were said to have been ritually slaughtered by the Jews. These stories arced back to England, and a new, even more influential, myth of Jewish ritual murder arose. In 1255, Jews were said to have crucified Hugh of Lincoln, who was soon dubbed a saint. No evidence connected the Jewish community with Hugh's death, but King Henry III retaliated against it by executing nineteen Jews.[25]

This supposed ritual murder would be immortalized in Chaucer's "The Prioress's Tale," one of the twenty-four stories of his *Canterbury Tales* (1478). Thanks to Chaucer's great literary fame, "The Prioress's Tale" lent credence to the notion that Jews killed Christian children as part of their religious rituals. But it was Thomas of Monmouth who had composed the original libel against the Jews, and the myth he created, concludes the historian Gavin Langmuir, "caused, directly or indirectly, far more deaths than William's [actual] murderer could ever have dreamt of committing."[26]

Since neither of the English ritual murder accusations involved the supposed Jewish need for Christian blood, the first real "blood libel" occurred on the European continent in the central German town of Fulda. On Christmas Day in 1235, five Christian boys died in a fire, and the local Jews were accused of killing them to harvest their blood. Three days later, thirty-four Jews were tortured and killed in retaliation. One chronicler said that the thirty-four were killed by crusaders from other parts of Germany, while another pinned the responsibility on the residents of Fulda. Word of these events spread quickly around the Holy Roman Empire (medieval Germany), and the emperor, Frederick II, felt compelled to intervene. After hearing testimony from prominent converted Jews, who told the emperor that the Bible and the Talmud forbade Jews to consume any blood, animal or human, Frederick ruled the accusation against the Jews of Fulda false. He warned his subjects not to repeat any such accusations in the future.

Not all of Frederick's subjects heeded the warning. In 1247,

Christian inhabitants in Valréas, a town on the western frontier of the empire, claimed that local Jews had crucified a Christian child and then used his blood in their religious rituals. Several Jews—it's unclear how many—were tortured and killed in punishment for their supposed crime. The survivors appealed to the pope, Innocent IV, who sharply condemned the killings when still more Jews were slaughtered after being charged with eating the heart of a Christian child for Passover. The pontiff issued a bull against the persecution of the Jews and specifically forbade the accusation that Jews engaged in what Langmuir calls "ritual cannibalism."[27] The pope did not, however, forbid accusations of ritual murder that alleged crucifixion rather than the consumption of blood.

The bull was thus equivocal, and a considerable number of Catholics would ignore it. From 1235 on, ritual murder accusations against Jews would essentially be "blood" libels, even if they also involved crucifixion or other forms of torture. But why the stepped-up persecution of the Holy Roman Empire's Jews in the thirteenth century, and why the new focus on blood? Langmuir offers three linked explanations: First, a precocious inquisition against perceived heretics surfaced there, and Jews were deemed the worst heretics of all; second, a new crusade roared through the empire in the thirteenth century, and Jews had long been a prime target of crusaders; third, heretics were said, at this time, to engage in satanic rituals involving orgies of fornication, incest, and ritual cannibalism. As for the new preoccupation with blood, Christians had come to believe in the magical and medicinal power of blood. But the crucial development of this period was the declaration in 1215 that transubstantiation was a dogma, a mandatory belief, of the Catholic Church.

Transubstantiation was, of course, the notion that during the ceremony of the Eucharist, bread and wine become—are consecrated as—the body and blood of Christ. In consuming both, communicants take Christ into themselves.

Langmuir shows that a fair number of Christians of the thirteenth century refused to believe that the Eucharist produced the real body and blood of Christ and that Church leaders resolved to stamp out this heresy.[28] Once Christian heretics had been suppressed, Jews were left as the ultimate heretics—no Muslims were available locally—and they bore the brunt of the persistent effort to enforce the dogma of transubstantiation.

The era's fascination with blood focused attention on the wine/blood half of the Eucharistic dyad and, in turn, on its Jewish deniers, a people believed to engage in satanic rituals featuring cannibalism. As these different strands of rumor and belief twisted together, the idea emerged that Jews, rejecting the Eucharist, used real blood instead of wine in their own rituals, and given as they were to cannibalism, had taken that blood from their Christian enemies and consumed it.

Why the blood had to come from children remains unclear in Langmuir's analysis. A potential answer to this question comes from the historian Israel Yuval, who maintains that Jewish as well as Christian beliefs and practices must be taken into account. His explanation begins with the First Crusade in 1096 when fighters bound for the Holy Land rampaged through Central Europe killing Jews and destroying their property. In the wake of these events, stories of Jewish suicides and of fathers killing their wives and children circulated throughout the region. In later centuries, these terrible deeds were explained as desperate efforts by Jews to prevent themselves and their children from being forcibly converted to Christianity. But during the generation after 1096, Jewish chroniclers glorified the suicides and the killing of children as acts of martyrdom designed to evoke God's vengeance against the devastation of the Crusades. Jews were angry over the contradiction between their biblical status as the Chosen People and the persistent reality of their oppression. After the Crusades, it seemed clear that the balance would be righted only in a future messianic age, and the Jews sought to hasten the coming of that age by stirring God to action. Jews were convinced, Yuval writes, "that the blood of the martyrs can rouse God to take messianic vengeance" against their Christian antagonists.[29]

Jewish self-sacrifice, including the sacrifice of their children, would also be a powerful way to atone for Jewish sins and bring about a divine Redemption. One particularly dramatic chronicle set during the Crusades featured a man, Isaac ben David, who converted to Christianity believing that by taking this action he would prevent the forced baptism of his children. But when he found his house untouched and his children unthreatened, he decided that his conversion was a sin so terrible that it could be atoned only though a ritual sacrifice, one that would impress God with his piety. He took his children to the synagogue and killed them before the Holy Ark, sprinkling their blood on the pillars that supported it. "May this blood," he declared, "be atonement for all my sins."[30]

Yuval acknowledges that cases of "Jews who killed themselves or their loved ones . . . were rare" but maintains that the Isaac ben David story and others like it strongly influenced not only the Jews' views about self-sacrifice but also Christians' understanding of Jewish behavior. "It seems doubtful," Yuval writes, "that Jewish acts of martyrdom were meant to shape Christian public opinion, but they were certainly known to Christians and had a great impact on them." When Christians got wind of these stories, they decided that if Jews could ritually spill the blood of their own children—an especially horrific act—they were all the more likely to spill the blood of Christian children. Christians, Yuval says, transformed the Jewish self-sacrifice, seen "as emphasizing the Jews' alleged great fondness for sacrificing children specifically," into an imagined ritual murder of the Christian young. This was, of course, a terrible distortion of Jewish practices and beliefs, but given the Christians' own messianic views, it made a certain twisted sense.[31]

It's more than plausible that Jews and Christians were aware of each other's beliefs while also misunderstanding and distorting them. But Yuval doesn't provide much evidence that the Jewish tales of self-sacrifice "had a great impact" on Christians—or even on Jews.[32] We don't know how the chronicles in question circulated, who had access to them, or whether they, in fact, seeped deeply into Christian communities. Nor do we know to what extent the chronicles narrated actual historical events. What's important, Yuval suggests, is not whether the chronicles conformed precisely to realities on the ground, which, given the existing sources, can't be known. What counts above all, Yuval says, is that the stories of Jewish self-sacrifice shaped the perceptions and beliefs of Jews and Christians alike.

This case seems more suggestive than definitive, and it raises the troubling possibility that Jewish practices contributed, however inadvertently, to the ritual murder myth. Another explanation of why Jews were said to target Christian children may have to do with the large number of stories about the Virgin

Mary and her miracles that had begun to circulate widely in the mid-twelfth century. In those stories, Jesus was always a child, and he tended to be perched on Mary's lap as the miracle unfolded. By the thirteenth century, artists commonly depicted Jesus as a child—far more than as an adult.[33] So, in the subconscious Christian mind, the Jews, in killing a Christian child and consuming the blood, symbolically eliminated the baby Jesus before he could grow up to preach against them. Jewish ritual murder thus enacted the symbolic destruction of Christianity, which is what made it an act that transcended the killing of an individual child, terrible as that was, to become the abolition of Christianity itself. This was the ultimate crime, and it required a fearsome, unrestrained response.[34]

For many of these reasons, the ritual murder accusation against the Jews, which after Fulda, generally took the form of a blood libel, became commonplace in medieval Europe. So did the charge of "host desecration," a blasphemy in which Jews were said to steal the sacred wafer, or host, of the Eucharist and then torture it, often with needles, until it bled. In the blood libel, the Jews were said to steal the blood of Christ-like children; in host desecration, they made Christ himself bleed, symbolically reenacting the Passion and the tortures that accompanied it.[35] Host desecration and the blood libel were tightly related to each other in that both appeared only after transubstantiation became a dogma of the Catholic Church. It is important to add that reports of ritual murders and host desecrations were always secondhand; no one ever saw Jews commit ritual murder or torture a host. Nor did Jews ever admit to committing these crimes unless subjected to judicial torture, which was common in the Middle Ages.

Throughout the thirteenth century and into the fourteenth and fifteenth, Jews faced accusations of ritual murder or host desecration every few years—in Baden (1267), Alsace (1270), Mainz (1283), Munich (1285), Berne (1294), Prague (1303), Cracow (1330), Pulka (1370), Posen (1401), Ems (1453), etc. Miracles of various kinds often followed the supposed murder or desecration, and in virtually every case, Jews, often in large numbers, were tortured and killed. Many of the blood libels took place around Passover, as Jews were said to require Christian blood to make matzo, but they occurred at other times as well. Jews supposedly cleansed themselves of sin by bathing in Christian blood, used it for their weekly Sabbath ceremonies, and considered it a cure for various diseases and disabilities, including impotence.[36]

Such regular accusations sparked the claim that in addition to their ritual murders, Jews poisoned the wells used by Christians. In retaliation for this supposed crime, roving bands of "Jew bashers" clubbed thousands of Jews to death. One of the worst massacres took place in Strasbourg in 1349, where some 2,000 Jews were burned alive. Before long, Jews organized themselves into armies of self-defense and retaliated against their attackers before succumbing, in most cases, themselves.

The disorder involved in this Christian/Jewish warfare horrified popes, kings, large landowners, and other powerful people. In some cases, as we have seen, the powers that be tried to restore order by denouncing or forbidding ritual murder accusations. These royal and papal prohibitions went largely ignored. Why? According to David Nirenberg, Christians of the medieval and early modern periods commonly saw kings, even popes, as being intimately tied to the Jews and complicit in their

crimes.[37] Kings, it was said, used Jews as fronts for usurious mon-
eylending and as tax collectors, and those Jews exploited nobles,
townsmen, and ordinary people on behalf of the king. Jews did
so at a time when kings enjoyed only a limited ability to impose
taxes and increase their wealth. The Jews, in this telling, thus
expanded the fiscal reach and political power of monarchs—and
of the Jews themselves—at the expense of everyone else.

To check these powers, prominent nobles, municipali-
ties, and representative bodies such as estates and parliaments
regularly punished individual Jews and disobeyed their king,
often labeling him "a Jew" or an agent of the Jews. In the mid-
fourteenth century, for example, a group of Castilian aristo-
crats deposed King Peter, calling him "king of the Jews" and
the illegitimate son of a Jewess. One of Peter's successors, Juan
II, would himself be denounced as "Jew-loving," as would the
man who overthrew him, his son Henry IV, accused not only of
privileging the Jews but of living like a Muslim. Even Ferdinand
and Isabel, the archetypal "Catholic monarchs" who expelled
hundreds of thousands of Jews and Muslims from their realm,
found themselves suspected of having Jewish ancestors and
being overly friendly to the Jews.[38]

Kings responded to such allegations by claiming that the
Jews belonged to them as a form of property, and therefore that
Jews held no power over them. The Holy Roman Emperor Frederick II added that such ownership required him to give "his"
Jews a measure of protection, which, in any case, Saint Augustine, referring to Psalm 59, had urged his contemporaries to do.
"Slay them not," Augustine wrote, "but scatter them in your
might, lest your people forget your Law." By this directive, the
theologian meant not that Jews should enjoy the same treat-

ment as Christians, but rather that Jews must be preserved as living testimony to all that was lacking in pre-Christian times, as "fossils" bearing witness to the progress toward salvation that Christians had made.[39]

If Frederick heeded this Augustinian directive, a great many other rulers, before and after him, did not. Or if they heeded it, they emphasized its punitive side. In 1146, Peter the Venerable, abbot of the Cluny monastery, accused France's King Louis VII of treating his Jews too well, and Louis denied the charge, citing Augustine. "Slay them not," Louis quoted, but added, "for God does not wish them to be entirely killed and altogether wiped out, but to be preserved for greater torment and reproach, like the fratricide Cain, in a life worse than death."[40]

Louis stood much closer than Frederick to the dominant premodern view of Jews. Most early Christians, the apostle Paul excepted, depicted Jews in extremely negative terms, and if anything, their medieval and early modern successors bathed them in an even harsher light. As Nirenberg shows, the Jews in question weren't for the most part actually existing Jewish people; rather, they emerged as ideas and representations in theological debates. Of course, these harsh representations often had terrible consequences for real human beings, as the history of the ritual murder accusation so vividly shows. But theologians and political figures didn't have to know or interact with actual Jews to perceive how evil and depraved they were.

Early Christians and their successors condemned the Jews for failing to acknowledge the divinity of Christ, for embracing a profane world of slavery and falsehood, rather than a spiritual world of freedom and truth. In Jesus, Christian theologists believed, the Jews saw only the flesh, and not the God; they killed him, mistaking Jesus for a mortal man. Not every early Christian went as far as Saint John Golden Mouth, named archbishop of Constantinople in 397 CE, but he was anything but a fringe figure. In his *Discourses Against the Jews*, John called them obstinate beasts whose "condition is no better than that of pigs or goats." Jews were so obstinate that they "are not fit for work; they are fit for killing." He quoted the Christ-figure of Luke 19:27 to support his views: "But as for my enemies, who did not want me to be king over them, bring them here and slay them."[41]

John Golden Mouth voiced such notions in large part in the belief that Jews posed an existential threat to Christianity. No matter that the Christian empire in which he lived had made Jews an oppressed minority nonthreatening to anyone. John represented Jews in this way because the theology in which he was immersed had taught him to characterize most dangers, real or imagined, as Jewish.[42] As Nirenberg shows, John's anti-Jewish venom emerged from debates among Christians, but his hostility, like that of many others after him, inevitably attached itself to actually existing Jews, shaping their lives for the worst.

Conditions for the Jews became especially dire in the twelfth century, when the discourse of anti-Judaism lost most of the Augustinian ambiguity that had portrayed Jews as a people at once to be protected and reviled. Now theologians, kings, and other powerful people saw little need to protect the Jews. In the mid-thirteenth century, the great English land baron Simon de Montfort expelled all Jews from his vast domains, which included the city of Leicester. When Montfort's aunt agreed to shelter some of the displaced, Robert Grosseteste, one of the most prominent theologians of the time, scolded her severely. The Jews, he wrote, as the murderers of Christ, merited only the barest subsistence and should never enjoy the protection of men like her nephew. At best, Jews should "work the earth laboriously" and only "for some little sustenance for their miserable lives." Anyone who did more for the Jews became complicit in their crimes.[43]

At about the same time, Charles IV, the Holy Roman Emperor, won his crown from a rival in part by granting several German cities, whose support he needed, the right to kill the Jews within their gates. The slaughter began immediately. Remaining Augustinian prohibitions may have prevented more widespread killings, but nothing stopped Jews from being expelled from their homelands. They were banned from England (1290), France (provisionally in 1182, definitively in 1394), Austria (1412), Spain (1492), Sicily (1493), Naples (1553), and various parts of Germany throughout the sixteenth century, by which time virtually no Jews were left in Central and Western Europe. These expulsions commonly won parliamentary assent. When King Edward I banned the Jews from England, Parliament rewarded him with the largest tax appropriation in medieval English history. Charles of Anjou, ruler of a duchy in western France, found himself similarly rewarded in 1289 when the local parliament granted him substantial new revenues in exchange for his expulsion of the Jews.[44] Parliaments granted such largesse not only because their king punished Jewish "crimes odious to God," but because banning the Jews seemed to them the best way to preserve public order. These expulsions not uncommonly came on the heels of one or more ritual murder accusations, which inevitably led to waves of violence that threatened to spread and even to escape the authorities' control.

What would become the paradigmatic case of the blood libel took place in Trent, then in the southern reaches of the Holy Roman Empire and now in northern Italy. In March 1475, a two-year-old boy was found dead, and residents of the town accused the Jews of brutally murdering him. We have detailed knowledge of this case thanks to a long narrative written at the time by the physician Giovanni Mattia Tiberino, who had examined the corpse of the child (later known as Simon of Trent).[45]

Unlike earlier accusations of ritual murder, which produced various forms of deadly vigilante justice, the Trent case, having occurred in a Renaissance Italy infused with humanistic ideas, led to a trial. The putative Jewish criminals were not simply to be put to death but rather tried in a court of law in which evidence would be gathered and weighed by magistrates. But in this Renaissance court, judges gathered the evidence through judicial torture. The magistrates had in mind a narrative of what the Jews had supposedly done, and the defendants endured grotesque tortures until they confessed to a series of terrible deeds and confirmed the narrative already in place. According to the story line developed by the court, the Jews' Passover ceremony featured the ritual murder of young Christian boys, who were cruelly cut and drained of their blood.[46]

Tiberino's text elaborated on the trial and added details and commentary to the judicial narrative of the supposed Jewish crime. The physician portrayed the Jews as so excited over the prospect of tasting Christian blood that strange, barbaric sounds poured from their mouths as they defiled the body of "glorious Simon, virgin martyr," whom they crucified "in contempt of

Simon of Trent. From *Passio beati Simonis* by Johannes Matthias Tuberinus, 1475. Church of Santa Maria Annunciata, Bienno, Italy.

our faith."[47] "Extending violently both of his sacred arms in the manner of the crucifix," Tiberino added, the Jews, "raising their weapons, sank them hard in the reclining sacred body." Like Jesus, Simon lowered "his head [as] he gave up his holy spirit to the Lord." By performing this horrible act, Tiberino added, the Jews expressed contempt for the "true religion" and denigrated Jesus Christ.

But the sacrifice of Simon, awful as it was, produced wondrous effects in the form of miracles and also in the condemnation and execution of the guilty Jews. With this punishment, Christianity triumphed over the Jewish efforts to denigrate it. And in exacting this Christian justice, the community of believers could see that God would, in the end, dispense divine justice to them. Simon's sacrifice, like Jesus' sacrifice, would allow them to be saved.[48]

The printing press, invented a quarter-century before the ritual murder trial in Trent, allowed Tiberino's account, published in multiple editions, to spread throughout the Holy Roman Empire. So influential was Tiberino's text that it etched the narrative grooves onto a record of ritual murder that would become the standard story repeated by antisemites from then on. That narrative added new justifications to the already intense persecution of European Jews; to escape the violence against them, Jews fled the Holy Roman Empire, the center of the era's nascent pogroms, for the more placid lands—at least at that time—of Poland, Lithuania, and Italy.

Newly arrived in Eastern or Southern Europe, Jews didn't remain safe for long: the ritual murder accusation followed them wherever they went, especially in Polish lands, where Jews settled in droves.[49] Between 1547 and 1787, eighty-two accusations of ritual murder victimized Jewish inhabitants of Poland, especially in Galicia and regions later annexed by Prussia. In 1713, a Polish priest named Stephan Zuchowski published a pamphlet entitled "A criminal Case about an Innocent Child," which repeated much of the narrative of Jewish ritual murder laid out in Trent nearly 250 years earlier. Only this time, the locale was Sandomierz in Poland. Zuchowski reinforced this narrative with a large dose of history, one that recounted the hundreds of supposed ritual murders committed by Jews since medieval times. Because they had murdered so many Christian children in the past, Zuchowski maintained, they must have done so again in the Polish present of the early eighteenth century.[50]

Following the Sandomierz case, the persecution of Polish Jews intensified until Jewish leaders appealed to Pope Clement XIII, who ruled in 1758 that the blood libel was just that: such accusations against Jews had no merit. In the wake of the Vatican's declaration, and the Polish parliament's outlawing of judicial torture in 1776, ritual murder accusations subsided. They had waned as well in Protestant Europe, where theologians rejected the idea that the bread and wine of the Eucharist became the body and blood of Christ. In most Protestant sects, bread and wine symbolized Christ rather than representing his real presence, so Protestants tended to worry neither about host desecration nor about a Jewish need to harvest the blood of Christ-like children.[51]

Despite the lull in blood libels, there is evidence that the belief in Jewish ritual murder had sunk deeply and indelibly into the memories of peasants, working people, and members of the middle class. Just because no open accusations occurred for a significant period of time didn't mean that the beliefs on which they were based had melted away. During the supposedly enlightened, scientific nineteenth century, the blood libel would surface again and again during times of political and economic stress. The blood libel resurfaced, writes the historian Hillel Kieval, because it resided in the collective memory of inhabitants of Central and Eastern Europe, where blood libels had been common between the thirteenth and eighteenth centuries.[52] These memories, however vague, created what Kieval calls a "social knowledge" about supposed Jewish behavior, and this knowledge was reinforced by a Catholic iconography designed to keep memories alive. The image, for example, of the "little Simonio," the child supposedly killed by the Jews of Trent, took the form of statues, paintings, plaques, frescoes, woodcuts, inscriptions, calendars, and texts regularly reproduced in Germany and Italy between the sixteenth and eighteenth centuries. A great many Catholics venerated these and other such images of ritual murder, and they built a number of religious rituals around them.[53]

That such memories of ritual murder persist doesn't mean they will blossom into full-blown anti-Jewish accusations—in most cases they won't. But during the tense decades of the late nineteenth century, the "social knowledge" of ritual murder bubbled back to the surface. It was then encouraged and embellished by traditionalist clergymen and antisemitic journalists and politicians eager to exploit local social knowledge for their religious and political ends.[54]

The historian Alain Corbin has documented the eruption of such social knowledge in 1870 in Hautefaye, a small, isolated town in southwestern France. In this case, the knowledge in question didn't refer to antisemitism but rather to the peasants' semi-repressed antagonism to nobles, priests, and republicans, an antagonism grounded in dormant memories of the French Revolution.[55] During the Franco-Prussian War of 1870, the Hautefaye peasants were terrified by the prospect of a Prussian invasion of their region, and their terror revived repressed memories of the foreign invasions of France during the French

Unknown, fifteenth century, *Martyrdom of the Blessed Simon of Trent.*
Fresco. Barbaine (Bs) chiesa di S. Andrea. Brescia, Italy.

Francesco Oradini, (1699–1754). *The Blessed Simon of Trent in Glory.* Relief on the façade of Palazzo Salvadori, Trent.

Revolution. Nobles and priests had been complicit in those invasions, and Hautefaye's peasants felt certain that they would be complicit once again. These peasants had voted overwhelmingly for Napoleon III in the elections of the 1850s and 1860s and believed he alone would shield them from the Prussian wrath. Since republicans opposed him, they were the peasants' enemies as well.

With France in danger of losing the war in the late summer of 1870, peasant fear boiled over into violence. During a local fair, rumors circulated that a resident nobleman, Alain de Moneys, was a Prussian, a republican, and a friend of the priests—a threefold enemy of the people. A group of peasants captured the young nobleman and tortured him for several hours, pushing him from one part of the fairground to the next, as if to the different stations of the cross. He died in agony as dozens of men, one after another, gradually finished him off.

When local and national officials accused de Moneys's murderers of barbarism befitting the Middle Ages rather than the enlightened nineteenth century, the peasants were stunned. From their point of view, they were protectors of a fatherland in danger, not murderers. The point of Corbin's story for our purposes is that rumors can emerge from dormant memories awakened during a period of sociopolitical, military, or economic strain. This is precisely what would happen throughout Europe in the late nineteenth century, as large numbers of people—especially farmers, artisans, and shopkeepers—found their livelihoods threatened by the long economic depression of the mid-seventies to the mid-nineties. These economic troubles dovetailed with fears on the part of religious traditionalists and other conservatives that society was changing too quickly, that capitalism and liberalism had disrupted once-stable values, and that the Jews, as exemplars of the liberal, capitalist economy, had become too influential. Such ideas awakened memories of tales recounting Jewish ritual murder and convinced people throughout Europe that Jews represented a danger to Christian life.

The United States experienced similar socioeconomic stress in the late nineteenth century, but nativists and traditionalists, having little experience with Jews in their midst, pinned no particular blame on them for the country's economic woes— although there were scattered complaints about "Jewish bankers." Instead, traditionalists held the ensemble of immigrant groups, including Jews, responsible, at least in part, for the economic depression and disorienting social change. The absence of any history of the blood libel in this country meant that there would be little social knowledge of supposed Jewish crimes to awaken amid the sharp anxieties and conflicts of the late nineteenth century, when labor unrest reached unprecedented heights and the lynching of African Americans left a toll of two dead every week.[56] There was prejudice against Jews, but it resembled the prejudice against members of the other non-Nordic ethnic groups entering the country—the Irish, Poles, Italians, Greeks, and Slavs, who were changing the demographic makeup of the United States. Eventually, however, that changing demography would help explain why the Massena blood libel occurred.

Chapter 2

BLOOD LIBEL IN THE MODERN WORLD

The absence in the United States of any social memory of ritual murder makes the Massena blood libel puzzling at best, especially since there are no other well-documented cases anywhere else in this county. It can be explained in part by the presence of large numbers of immigrant workers who had come from places in Europe and Canada where the ritual murder accusation—and its social memory—had been all too common in the late nineteenth and early twentieth centuries.

In Europe, the countries in question were Germany, Austria-Hungary, Russia, Greece, and Romania, among others. Germany saw an episode of the blood libel already early in the nineteenth century. In 1819, a young girl disappeared in the village of Dormagen in western Prussia, and even before anyone discovered a body, local Jews found themselves accused of ritual murder.

Dormant social knowledge about the Jews had been awakened during the severe economic contraction of the years following the Napoleonic wars, an economic contraction that had already sparked anti-Jewish rioting across a wide swathe of German-speaking Europe. As one local writer put it, "The prevailing [opinion] is that the Jews captured the child because at times, *according to an old legend* [italics added], they must have Christian blood."[1] The "old legend" recalled the death in a nearby village of a young boy supposedly murdered by the Jews more than 500 years earlier. The legend had been kept alive, if subliminally, in popular literature, religious iconography, and local rituals.[2]

Perhaps the most serious blood libel of the early nineteenth century unfolded over a dozen years in Velizh, a small town in western Russia.[3] On Easter Sunday in 1823, two young cousins, three-year-old Fedor and four-year-old Avdotia, went for a walk. Only Avdotia came back. The four-year-old didn't know what had happened to his younger cousin, and his mother and other family members searched for Fedor in vain. Several days later, a neighbor found Fedor's mutilated body half buried in a marsh. Someone had moved the corpse there from the actual murder scene, and it was clear that the child had suffered a slow, agonizing death. He had deep puncture wounds on his arms, hands, knees, and even the top of his head, suggesting that the killer or killers had repeatedly stabbed him with nails. His feet, stomach, arms, and head had been scrubbed raw with a stiff brush or cloth. As in other similar cases, rumors began to fly accusing Velizh's Jews of murdering the child. The Jews vehemently denied the accusation, and in the absence of any hard evidence or credible eyewitness accounts, the local magistrates ruled that there had been no ritual murder.

The story did not end here, however. In 1825, Tsar Nicolas, en route to a seaside vacation, passed through Velizh, where one Maria Terenteeva handed him a note that repeated the dismissed ritual murder charge. Terenteeva was an indigent townswoman who claimed to have unwittingly participated in the crime, although her earlier accusations had not swayed the local court. But the tsar took her seriously and had his judicial officials reopen the case. After a lengthy investigation, forty-three Jews were charged with ritual murder and also with the then-serious crime of forcibly converting Terenteeva and two other women to Judaism.

The arrested Jews were held in horrible conditions and interrogated harshly; eventually some began to crack. Their stories wavered in ways that seemed suspicious to the investigators, who noted that the majority of Velizh's Christian residents appeared convinced that the Jews had done the terrible deed. In the end, about three dozen Jews were sentenced to exile in Siberia and to a public knouting, or flogging with a braided leather whip, the worst form of corporal punishment allowed in tsarist Russia.

The case had gone on for more than eight years, but still it wasn't done. Although senators representing the region believed that Jews committed ritual murder, some were troubled by the absence of any confessions by the Jews said to have killed Fedor. These senators sent the matter up to Russia's State Council, the administrative body that stood between the Senate and the tsar. On January 18, 1835, almost twelve years after Fedor's death, the State Council reversed the convictions. The tsar, however, proved reluctant to completely absolve the Jews. Although he agreed that there was insufficient legal proof against them, he did not, as he put it, have the "inner conviction that the murder has not been committed by Jews."[4] Fortunately, Russian law and administrative procedure kept most elements of the case secret, and given the lack of anything resembling a free press, this ritual murder accusation remained unpublicized and largely unknown to the wider society. Unlike certain later instances, the Jews of Velizh would not suffer from popular violence once the case was closed.

If Germans were unaware of Velizh, many remembered Dormagen. New ritual murder accusations—with corresponding violence against Jews—popped up in Germany as the century went on: Neuenhoven in 1834, Willich in 1835, Bavaria in 1845, Cologne in 1861, Eniger in 1873. These were all Catholic areas, as a religious revival in Catholic Germany recalled the conflicts of the Middle Ages. Public officials, committed to rational, orderly government and society, largely contained the anti-Jewish violence, even if they failed to stamp out the "medieval" outbursts themselves.[5]

As troubling as these episodes were, they paled in comparison to the wave of blood libels that accompanied the severe economic downtown of the late nineteenth century—not only in Germany, but throughout Europe. In the last decade of the century alone, observers documented seventy-nine cases of the blood libel. The Dual Monarchy of Austria-Hungary (today consisting of those two countries plus the Czech Republic, Slovakia, Slovenia, Croatia, Bosnia-Herzegovina, and parts of Italy, Romania, Ukraine, and Poland) led the ignominious list with nearly half (thirty-six) of the anti-Jewish accusations. Germany came in second with fifteen, followed by Bulgaria (eleven), Russia (five), Romania (two), Greece (two), Serbia (one), and France (one), among others.[6] The early twentieth century would see several more—most notoriously in Konitz, Germany (1900), and Kiev, Ukraine (1911).[7]

In many of these cases, the original accusation emerged from local social knowledge, but since this was the fin de siècle, the heyday of modern print journalism, accusations were nurtured and embellished in antisemitic newspapers, pamphlets, and books. Journalists elaborately covered the blood libels and the trials they regularly produced, spreading biased and patently false information about them to a now largely literate European population. One anti-Jewish accusation easily triggered others, especially since journalists and other writers possessed the means to teach people throughout Europe to see the death, or even disappearance, of any Christian child as the work of the Jews.

This new flood of blood libels coincided with a wave of anti-Jewish violence unprecedented since the Middle Ages. The violence began in Russia in 1881 after terrorists, some of them Jewish, assassinated Tsar Alexander II. The assassination may have sparked the rioting, but it was far from its only cause. A key factor was an explosive growth of the Russian-Jewish population that had begun earlier in the century and produced a widespread worry among Christians that Jews were becoming too powerful a group. Between 1820 and 1880, Russia's Jewish population increased by 150 percent while the overall population grew by only 87 percent. In the middle of the nineteenth century, Jews represented 3 percent of Russia's population; by the end of the century, that had ballooned to 9 percent. The

Jewish demographic explosion was even more dramatic in certain key regions to which Jews emigrated during the nineteenth century. Between 1844 and 1914, the Jewish population of Russia's southern provinces expanded by 850 percent, more than three times faster than the non-Jewish population. In Russian Poland during a slightly longer time period, the Jewish numbers climbed by 822 percent and the Jewish share of this region's inhabitants nearly doubled from 7.8 to 15 percent.[8]

These growing Jewish numbers threatened the non-Jewish population, who saw the Jews as a foreign, invasive force that would one day overtake them in size and influence. The supposed problem wasn't just the mounting Jewish numbers; it was also their "alien" culture—whether the culture of traditionalist Jews, with their Yiddish language, distinctive dress, and peculiar religious habits, or the culture of Westernized Jews, said to threaten genuine Russian ways with their liberal and socialist politics, their modernist art and literature, their commitment to competitive, atomistic capitalism. Peasants, in particular, worried that the Jews would soon dominate them economically. These fears dovetailed with long-standing religious animosities so that when the tsar was killed, many Russians blamed the Jews and decided to make them pay.[9]

The rioting began in urban centers to which Jews had emigrated en masse and where rapid economic change had disrupted the social order. Only later did peasants join in, hoping to share in the looting of Jewish property underway in the cities. The violence had not been encouraged by the Russian authorities, as many Jews thought at the time—and historians since—but rather erupted semi-spontaneously from local conditions. The rioting was only semi-spontaneous because traditionalist nobles had boosted it, as had businessmen and shopkeepers, who hoped to rid themselves of Jewish competition.[10]

The result was devastating for Russia's Jews, who faced more than 250 pogroms in the southern part of the country alone. This vast wave of violence killed a large number of Jews, destroyed thousands of homes and businesses, and decimated hundreds of communities.[11]

The Russian pogroms proved contagious: anti-Jewish violence spread in the 1880s and 1890s to Austria-Hungary and eastern Germany. In Galicia, a Polish part of the Dual Monarchy, pogroms engulfed more than four hundred Jewish communities, as bands of peasants looted Jewish shops and taverns, ransacked Jewish homes, and battered men, women, and children. The root social, economic, and cultural causes resembled those of Russia, but here ritual murder accusations played a larger role.

Shortly before the riots broke out, a Polish priest named Mateus Jez published a series of articles in a local paper alerting Christians to the supposedly huge number of ritual murders committed by Jews, and not just in Galicia. Jez drew on a wide variety of writings by European antisemites to show his readers just how much the Jews, wherever they lived, required the blood of Christian children.[12] Jez collected these articles into a pamphlet and distributed thousands of copies in exactly the regions where the pogroms would take place. In one town, a bank clerk egged on his neighbors by declaring, "The Jews have drunk enough of our blood, it is time to make an end to them."[13]

This rioter had doubtless been inspired by tales of recent, spectacular ritual murder trials in and around the Dual Monarchy, including Romania next door, and splashed across the

European press.[14] The most famous of these trials unfolded in Hungary over six weeks in the summer of 1883. The previous year, at Eastertime, a fourteen-year-old girl named Eszter Solymosi had abruptly disappeared from Tiszaeszlár, a small village northeast of Budapest. The girl's mother, Mária Solymosi, announced to neighbors and friends that her daughter had been the victim of Jewish ritual murder, even though there was no evidence she had died, let alone been murdered.

At first, the charge was ignored by local authorities, who found it bizarre. Jews were unusually well integrated into Hungarian society and in many ways faced less discrimination than their counterparts in Europe's most liberal countries, Britain and France. If anything, the Hungarian governments of the 1870s and 1880s could be considered philosemitic.[15] Antisemitic parties and politicians emerged in Hungary only after thousands of traditionalist Jews landed there, having fled difficult conditions in Russia.[16]

Why then did the blood libel emerge in Hungary in 1882? A deep-rooted social knowledge about ritual murder provides part of the answer—a necessary but not sufficient ingredient of the full explanation. Only after antisemites made a concerted effort to nurture and reinforce that social knowledge did anguish over a missing child turn into a widely believed accusation against the Jews.

Shortly after Eszter went missing, her mother ran into Jószef Sharf, sexton of the Tiszaeszlár synagogue, whose efforts to console Mária aroused her suspicions; he seemed to protest too much. She quickly decided that Jószef must have been involved in the death of her daughter, testifying later that her suspicions had been divinely inspired and then confirmed in a dream. Another way to put it would be that Mária's latent knowledge, or memories, about the Jews had been tapped. She told her son to hunt for Eszter's grave and demanded that the police arrest József Sharf. In the absence of a body or any evidence of foul play, the local authorities dismissed her story out of hand.[17]

Mária remained convinced of Sharf's guilt and resolved to investigate further, asking other village women to join in a search for evidence to confirm her belief. They approached Sharf's five-year-old son Samu, who gave them what they were looking for. One of the women said she had overheard Samu tell his friends that his father had enticed Eszter to the synagogue, where he tied her down, washed her, and then had her cut by the man who slaughtered animals for kosher meat. Samu implicated his older brother, the thirteen-year-old Móric, claiming, according to one of Mária's friends, that Móric had helped hold Eszter down as his elders butchered her alive.

The authorities were skeptical of such secondhand accounts of what a five-year-old may have said. But when Móric chimed in to corroborate his brother's story—although adding that he had been involved only as an observer—the situation abruptly changed. Móric said that he had looked through the keyhole of the synagogue door and saw his father and several other men tie Eszter to a chair, slit her throat, and collect her blood.[18]

There would be considerable conflict at the trial—and afterwards—over whether Móric's testimony had been coerced by an overzealous József Bary, the magistrate in charge of the pretrial investigation. Bary had sequestered Móric from his family for over a year, and the Jews and their Christian allies claimed that the magistrate had unduly influenced the boy. Bary said he had sequestered Móric for his own protection; his father and other village Jews had repeatedly threatened to harm him if he failed to change his story. It's unclear what Móric's motives may have been. Was his testimony just the latest installment in a long-standing conflict with his father? Was he somehow ashamed of being a Jew? Mentally or emotionally disturbed? Brainwashed by the investigating magistrate? In any event, Bary was dismissed from the case before it went to trial.

In the meantime, other Christian villagers filled in the story of ritual murder. Most damningly, they maintained that on the day Eszter disappeared, they had heard the muffled screams of a child coming from the synagogue.[19] Taken together, the claims of the Sharf boys, plus those of several village women, recapitulated much of what had become, since the fifteenth century, the standard script of ritual murder: at the time of Easter and Passover, a group of Jews kidnapped a Christian child, took him or her to the synagogue, and in a ceremony there, cut the child's throat. The body was then drained of blood for making matzo or for various other Jewish needs. In this script, seemingly lodged in social memory— of Christians and Jews alike—and now widely available in printed form, evidence for the terrible deeds came either from renegade Jews, converted Jews, children or mentally or emotionally deficient Jews, or from Jews who were marginal in some other way.

Of course, Mária Solymosi and the other accusers didn't think they were following an implicit script, nor did the Hungarian officials who now, in the wake of Móric's statements, took the accusation of ritual murder seriously. They charged thirteen Tiszaeszlár Jews with crimes in connection with Eszter Solymosi's disappearance—four with first-degree murder, five as accomplices to murder, and four as conspiring to cover up the crime.[20]

Complications arose on June 18, 1882, ten weeks after Eszter's disappearance, when a body washed up on the shores of the Tisa River. The corpse was decomposed and hard to recognize, but it was wearing Eszter's clothes. Since there was no wound to the neck or throat, the Jews and their allies said that Móric's story was false; there had clearly been no ritual murder. But Mária and several others who knew Eszter, including several doctors, said the body in question couldn't be hers. It was a much older woman, either married or a prostitute, as the physicians who examined the corpse found evidence of frequent sexual activity; the fourteen-year-old Eszter was a virgin, villagers said. In addition, the examiners claimed that the forensic evidence revealed that the woman was well-to-do and Jewish— the lack of hair on the body proved as much.[21]

From these supposed facts, the proponents of ritual murder concluded that another body of about Eszter's size had been substituted for her mutilated one and hastily dumped into the water. These conclusions seemed to be confirmed by the boatmen, some of them Jews, who had found the body. When questioned, they said that Jews from Tiszaeszlár had given it to them. These answers were contested during the trial as having been coerced. The Jews' defense attorney also maintained that the initial forensic analysis of the body was wrong. The more sophisticated analysis done for him showed that the body could easily have been of a fourteen-year-old.

Eszter's death was likely an accident, the defense said, not a murder of any kind.

Even before the trial opened on June 19, 1883, the putative ritual murder at Tiszaeszlár had become an explosive international affair. It took center stage at the first meeting of the Congress for Safeguarding of Non-Jewish Interests in Dresden, Germany, in September 1882. The congress brought together the major figures of Europe's nascent antisemitic parties and movements, which in Germany, Austria, and France were destined for a particularly bright future. Hungary's representatives, Győző Istóczy and Géza Ónody, played a major role in this event, and both milked the ritual murder charge in Tiszaeszlár for all it was worth. Istóczy, a lawyer elected to the Hungarian parliament in the early 1870s, hailed from a well-to-do landowning family. He became his country's lone prominent antisemitic politician and polemicist. Shortly after the 1882 congress, Istóczy published a "Manifesto to the Governments and Peoples of the Christian States Menaced by Organized Jewry." Ónody, for his part, happened to be Tiszaeszlár's representative to the Hungarian parliament, and he gave the congress's keynote address.

In his speech, Ónody claimed that Jews were pouring into Hungary and the lands that surrounded it with the goal of exploiting the local peasantry and eventually the country at large. The ritual murder they committed at Tiszaeszlár, he said, conformed to the directives of the Talmud and was intended to undermine traditional Hungarian society while subverting its judicial system. Ónody concluded his remarks by declaring, "The affair no longer involves just a single village, canton, or even Hungary itself, but rather the entire human race."[22]

While Ónody spoke, the audience could see a veiled painting standing off to his side. As he concluded his remarks, he yanked off the veil to reveal an angelic Eszter Solymosi. The portrait, Ónody said, captured her exact likeness, although it wasn't painted until after her death and no photographs existed. "You see before you," the orator declared, "that young girl whose

Eszter Solymosi

innocent soul took its last breath in the dark den of criminal madness belonging to the butchers of ritual crime."[23]

After the antisemitic congress, Ónody would play a major role in publicizing the charges against the Jews of the village he represented. He gained access to the supposedly secret pretrial investigation—the equivalent of an American grand-jury proceeding—and published the most apparently damning elements of it in Hungary's antisemitic newspaper, the *Függetlenség*. These dispatches were translated into German and collected into a pamphlet, which sold some 10,000 copies. The Jews' liberal defenders published their responses only later, which enabled the antisemites to shape the narrative of the affair.[24]

Besides Ónody and Istóczy, several Germans played a key role in prosecuting the Jews of Tiszaeszlár in the court of public opinion. The antisemitic theologian August Rohling, professor of Catholic theology at the German University of Prague, claimed expertise in the history of Judaism and argued, baselessly, that passages in the Talmud explained the Jews' penchant for ritual murder. Rohling's work had strongly influenced Europe's budding antisemitic movement, and he served as a consultant for the prosecution in the Tiszaeszlár case. His interventions, and those of other budding antisemites, adroitly connected two forms of Jew-hatred, one ancient, one modern. The ancient one is, of course, the blood libel; the modern version features the notion, invented by antisemites around the time of the Tiszaeszlár trial, that an international Jewish conspiracy exists to bring down Christian society.[25]

When the trial opened in June 1883, journalists from all over Europe and the Americas were there to cover it. To defend the thirteen Jews accused of murder or conspiracy, Jewish leaders from Budapest engaged Károly Eötvös, one of their country's most accomplished non-Jewish attorneys. Eötvös skillfully demonstrated the extent to which the pretrial investigation had been compromised, with witnesses pressured or coerced to uphold the narrative of ritual murder. In one of the trial's most dramatic moments, Eötvös led a field trip to Tiszaeszlár's synagogue, where Móric Sharf said he had watched the ritual murder through a keyhole. When the defense attorney had magistrates and witnesses peer through the keyhole, it quickly became clear that they couldn't see the inside of the sanctuary; Móric had invented his "eyewitness" account.

As the trial unfolded, the prosecutor became so convinced of the Jews' innocence that he seemed to join Eötvös in their defense, urging the court to declare them not guilty. In the end, the three judges absolved the five Jews charged with conspiracy, ruling them "not guilty." But they failed to fully exonerate those accused of murder, deciding only that the government's charges were "not proved." This ambiguous outcome enabled antisemites to argue afterwards that the prosecutor had been biased in favor of (or bought off by) the Jews, which is why he failed to prove his case. The Jews were guilty as charged, the antisemites declared.[26]

During the sixteen months between the original accusation and the conclusion of the trial, antisemites had agitated relentlessly for a guilty verdict, apparently convincing large numbers of people. When all thirteen Jews charged in the case were set free, riots broke out all around the country, with Hungary's Jews as the target. Hundreds were assaulted, their stores looted and synagogues vandalized. Polemicists maintained that the trial's "unjust" outcome showed that Jews had established de facto control over Hungarian society and politics and that something had to be done. As if to confirm this notion, the government, fearing disorder, intervened to stem the rioting. In response, Istóczy launched the National Anti-Semitic Party, anticipating the creation, slightly later, of powerful, mass-based antisemitic parties in Germany and Austria. When other major ritual murder accusations emerged—Xanten in the Prussian Rhineland (1891–92), Polná in Bohemia (1899–1900), Konitz in Prussia (Chojnice, Poland today, 1900–1901), and Kiev in Ukraine (1911–13)—organized antisemitism was ready to pounce.

Each of these cases, and several other smaller ones, resulted in widespread violence against Jews. There is no need to fully narrate each accusation; the story, with just a few modifications and local details, is always the same. In Xanten, townsmen found the body of a five-year-old boy whose throat had been slit. The body, it was said, had been drained of blood—evidence that supposedly pointed to the Jews, and especially to the kosher butcher Adolph Buschhoff. At this point, other Christian inhabitants chimed in: they had seen Buschhoff in an agitated state, heard him saying the Jews had to cover up the murder, observed his daughter wrap the body in her apron (instead of dumping it in a sack, as elsewhere) before hiding it. Such "evidence" proved sufficient to jail Buschhoff and provoke a chorus of anti-Jewish condemnation from the local and national antisemitic press, including Catholic and conservative newspapers, increasingly antisemitic at the end of the century. When government investigators came to Xanten to look into the crime, they found the case against him without merit and said so in court. After enduring a ten-day trial, Buschhoff was declared not guilty.

For antisemites, the verdict showed that the Jews, obviously guilty of ritual murder, now dominated the Prussian government. As in Tiszaeszlár, a wave of anti-Jewish assaults, desecration, and property damage ensued, its most creative feature a series of "large blood red crosses" placarded onto Jewish homes.[27] A Catholic butcher apparently confessed privately to the murder a few years later but was never charged.[28]

In Polná, at century's end, the victim was older than usual, a nineteen-year-old woman, but the rest of the story conformed to the script: at Passover time, villagers discovered a body. The throat had been slit and the body drained of blood. Near the body, townsmen found a knife said to be used in the kosher slaughter of animals; shortly afterwards, a renegade or disreputable Jew corroborated the accusation. Sadly, in this case, the falsely imprisoned Jew, Leopold Hilsner, having been threatened with lynching in jail, confessed to the murder to avoid being strung up. He retracted the confession in court but was convicted nonetheless and sentenced to death, later commuted to life in prison. Thomas Masaryk, destined to be Czechoslovakia's first president in 1918, came to Hilsner's defense, finding, to no avail, that the young woman in question had most likely been killed during a family quarrel over an inheritance.[29]

Kieval argues that press accounts of this "Jewish crime" took on a dark, racial tone absent in the classic medieval accounts but increasingly common in the late nineteenth century. Journalists described Hilsner "as an unkempt, unshaven, dark stranger, who was simultaneously sinister (black), deformed (hobbled) and effeminate (knock-kneed and unable to grow a beard)."[30] His appearance marked him as racially different, inferior, and a danger to Christian civilization. His menace came not entirely from his religion, admittedly hostile to Christians and Christianity, but from physical characteristics that marked him as indelibly different from the genuine Czech citizens of good racial stock. This racialist depiction of Hilsner conforms to the tropes invented in the 1870s by the modern mass press, which focused obsessively on crime and portrayed criminals as genetically different from normal people, as atavistic human forms that resembled primitive men more than modern ones.[31]

In Konitz, Germany, the supposed Jewish murderer, like the one in Xanten, was a kosher butcher, skilled in draining the blood from animals—and also, in the case of Konitz, in the putative ability to meticulously carve a carcass or body into pieces, the better to hide it.[32] In Kiev, a random Jew, Mendel Beilis, found himself accused of murdering a thirteen-year-old boy, Andrei Yushchinsky, for ritual purposes and cutting the child to harvest his blood. Nothing linked Beilis to the crime save for the proximity of his workplace to the cave where the boy's body was found.

As in the earlier European cases, organized antisemites jumped into the Ukrainian fray. For Andrei's funeral, they printed leaflets saying, "The kikes have tortured Andryusha to death!" The evidence against Beilis was even thinner than in most other ritual murder cases, which took place in villages and small towns, where Jews and non-Jews knew one another and interacted, even if they would have preferred not to.[33] Residing in Kiev, a large capital city, Beilis had no connection of any kind to the murdered boy. But he was a Jew, and that was all that mattered to the antisemites who howled for his head and the government officials who imprisoned him under horrid conditions before putting him on trial.

The case against him proved so weak that the mostly peasant jurors, expected to docilely endorse the prosecution's argument, ruled Beilis not guilty. Even so, they said that a ritual murder had indeed taken place—it was just that Beilis hadn't done it. Beilis's defenders had won a measure of justice for their innocent client, but Russia's antisemites felt vindicated in their belief that a Jewish ritual murder had taken place.

The outcome of the case resulted in predictable violence against Russia's Jews, but even in countries that managed to avoid assaults against Jews and destruction of their homes, businesses, and synagogues, the rhetorical violence against Jews became extreme in the late nineteenth century. Such was especially true of Italy and France, where traditionalist Catholics, hostile to the liberal values they associated with European Jews, avidly took up the theme of ritual murder as part of a larger antisemitic campaign.

In Italy, two key Catholic newspapers, Rome's La Civiltà Cattolica (Catholic Civilization) and Milan's L'Osservatore Cattolico (Catholic Observer), led the charge. The two papers, founded in 1850 and 1864, respectively, ardently supported the institutional authority of Pope Pius IX (1846–78) and his brand of ultra-traditionalist Catholicism, which posited papal infallibility and opposed liberalism, rationalism, and secularism, the hallmarks of the nineteenth century. They denounced Italy's new, unified secular state, which came together between 1860 and 1870 and granted full emancipation to Jews. Traditionalist Catholics took this acceptance as a reward of sorts for the Jews' supposed efforts to wrest Italy away from the pope and enshrine secular rule. In response, the two papers launched a vicious antisemitic campaign.

Civiltà's crusade featured a decades-long series of articles intended to prove that the ritual murder of Christian children played a central, essential role in the Jewish religion. Every year for Passover, the paper claimed, Jews murdered Christian children in obedience to the Talmud's commands. They needed young Christian blood to mix with Passover wine and as a key ingredient in matzo. But that wasn't all: the ritual diabolically reenacted the passion and death of Jesus and had to be as cruel and bloody as possible. The child was bound alive to a table and pierced repeatedly until all the blood had drained. Death came slowly and excruciatingly for the martyred victim.

To lend credence to these assertions, *Civiltà* detailed one ritual murder accusation after another beginning with Damascus in 1840, where Jews were said to have killed an Italian monk. It then narrated supposed ritual murders in Alexandria and Port Said, Egypt, in 1881 and 1882 and gave elaborate, sensationalistic accounts of the Tiszaeszlár case and, later, the trials in Xanten, Polná, and Kiev. In each instance, Jews' guilt was "established beyond doubt."[34] For added journalistic heft, the paper published a list of sixty ritual murders between 1071 and 1891. To seal its case against the Jews, the Catholic paper cited the writings of religious authorities such as Rohling and, for putative authenticity, the claims of certain converted Jews—former rabbis, the paper said, who had ultimately seen the religious light. "It is in vain," the editors declared, "that Jews seek to slough off the weight of argument against them."[35]

While *Civiltà* focused on the putative evils of Jewish religious practice, the *Osservatore Cattolico* concentrated on the Jews' more secular crimes—while not neglecting ritual murder. In 1885, *Osservatore*'s editor Davide Albertario wrote, "The

Jew is lord of gold," and because gold is now supreme, "the Jew is the universal ruler," the masters, he added, of Italy, Austria-Hungary, Germany, and France. Worse, the Jews had imported liberalism into Italy and used it to dominate "parliament, journalism, and the family, yes, everything."[36]

Albertario turned to the blood libel after the German Protestant theologian Hermann L. Strack published a book in 1891 criticizing the ritual murder accusation, which he called a "terrible disease of superstitious belief."[37] To challenge Strack's impeccable, ultra-scholarly work, the *Osservatore* began a two-year-long campaign to establish the truth of Jewish ritual murder, at one point publishing two articles a week. In these pieces, Albertario rehearsed the now-standard list of the Jews' ritual crimes and claimed that the more Jews denied the accusations against them, the more their guilt shone through.[38] With this argument, Albertario put his finger on a major problem for Europe's Jews: the cascade of accusations and the trials that followed trapped them in an impossible argument about ritual murder. Jews were forced to prove a negative, which was virtually impossible to do, especially in the presence of a child's mutilated body.[39]

In Italy, the obsession with ritual murder came mainly from conservative Catholics; in France, it ranged more widely from populists to Catholics and seeped into the mainstream of French political life. Like their German and Austrian counterparts, French antisemites came out with a new, toxic brew epitomized by Edouard Drumont's lengthy anti-Jewish polemic, *La France juive* (Judaized France, 1886). Drumont's book became a massive bestseller, exhausting 140 editions within its first two years and ultimately selling a million copies by the eve of the First World

War.[40] Spurred by his publishing success, Drumont founded an antisemitic daily, *La libre parole* (Free Speech, 1892), which by the time of the Dreyfus Affair two years later, had become one of France's most popular newspapers—circulation 200,000.

Jesuits and other conservative Catholics helped finance Drumont's endeavors and encouraged him to turn his diffuse Jew-hatred into a form of racism. The French polemicist described Jews as characterized by their "famous hooked nose, blinking eyes, a clenched jaw, protuberant ears, square nails, flat feet, round knees [and] a soft and flabby hand of the hypocrite and traitor."[41] All Jews, he added, "had a stinking odor," and because they were "perpetual nomads," could never be French, no matter how assimilated they became—or even if they converted to Christianity.[42]

Like Rohling, Drumont blamed the Talmud for the evils of the "Jewish race."[43] This sacred text, he said, required Jews to hate Christians and Christianity and to commit ritual murder. Jews had murdered Christian children for a millennium, but now, in the late nineteenth century, they were especially dangerous because their emancipation during the French Revolution and afterwards had allowed them to insinuate themselves into all aspects of European society. Ultimately, they would "achieve complete mastery over non-Jews" through their control of the press, the economy, and the French republic, a corrupt, liberal regime in which Protestants and Masons had given Jews the keys to the city.

Drumont's *Judaized France* spawned a number of imitators, and for the major ones, he wrote the preface. These titles included three books by Henri Desportes: *Christian Blood in the Rites of the Modern Synagogue* (1888), *The Mystery of Blood in Jew-*

ish Life Since the Beginning (1889), and *Killed by the Jews: History of a Ritual Murder* (1890). In his preface to the last of the three, Drumont wrote that ritual murder could not be relegated to the past; Jews were still doing it in the late nineteenth century, especially in Catholic countries. As for Desportes himself, he claimed that ritual murder was still "practiced by the entire Jewish people."[44]

To prove their contention, the two writers heavily publicized a ritual murder that had supposedly taken place in Damascus in October 1890, and they placarded Paris with posters warning Christian mothers to keep their young children close. They added that the only way to stop the plague of Jewish killing was to expel all Jews or confine them to ghettoes. When France's Jewish leaders asked their Catholic counterparts to condemn such inflammatory remarks, they were met with silence. Not until 1907 did any top Catholic clergymen denounce the ritual murder charge.

By the time of the Dreyfus Affair (1894), when a Jewish army captain was falsely accused of selling military secrets to the Germans, antisemitic writers had embellished the now-commonplace script of ritual murder. Not only, the antisemites said, did Jews need Christian blood for Passover matzo, it was a crucial ingredient of hamentaschen, the distinctive pastries made for Purim, the Jewish holiday celebrated shortly before Passover. Jews, the antisemites maintained, cynically gave the pastries to Christians as a gift.[45]

Most French antisemitic writers portrayed Jews as a racial rather than a religious group and, as such, they couldn't ever be loyal French citizens. A book by one A. Puig, which took third place in the *Libre Parole*'s essay contest of 1896, described Jews as a "degenerate race," as "vampires," "serpents," "vipers born of the Devil," and "vermin of humanity."[46] Such racial antisemitism filled the columns of France's two main Catholic newspapers, *La Croix* (The Cross), circulation 200,000, and *Le Pèlerin* (The Pilgrim), circulation 140,000. During the Xanten ritual murder trial in 1892, their rhetoric about this "Jewish crime" became so violent that France's chief rabbi, Zadoc Kahn, dropped his characteristic reserve and refuted it in public. The *Libre Parole* published Kahn's critique on its front page, happy to ridicule him the following day.[47]

Although France's rhetoric of antisemitism became at least as intense as elsewhere in Europe, the country's liberal, republican government mostly kept the lid on violence against Jews and ultimately exonerated Dreyfus in 1908, fourteen years after his arrest. The great exception was French Algeria, which Drumont represented in the French National Assembly and where powerful anti-Jewish rioting broke out in the wake of the Dreyfus Affair. France's colonial officials did little to squelch the violence, and Algeria's sizable Jewish community suffered cruelly.[48] Even though France produced no ritual murder trials during the volatile late nineteenth century—the Dreyfus case perhaps substituted for them—the accusation that Jews regularly killed Christian children received widespread publicity in the antisemitic and Catholic press, and it's likely that a great many French men and women believed it.

The echoes of French antisemitism would reverberate in French Canada, whose borders stood just a few miles from Massena, New York. A fair number of French Canadians had migrated to the upstate town in search of the industrial jobs on offer there. And many of these Québécois would have been aware of the ritual murder charges against the Jews, both in France and in their own province, as would Massena's European immigrants. Many had come in the early twentieth century from the very countries where the most notorious blood libels had taken place.

Chapter 3

WHO DONE IT: THE IMMIGRANTS?

Although Mayor Hawes and Corporal McCann had given official credence to the idea that Massena's Jews had committed ritual murder, when confronted by the rabbi, they tried to pin the blame on others, either unnamed "foreigners" or one of the many French Canadians in town. The existence of a large number of immigrants—nearly a third of Massena's population in 1930 was foreign-born—lent a certain credibility to the idea that one or more "foreigners" were responsible for the accusation against the Jews. Massena's residents had come from Poland, Hungary, Russia, Romania, and Greece—precisely the countries in which sensational ritual murders had supposedly taken place. Nearly 200 of the immigrants listed in the 1930 census hailed from Italy, where leading Catholic newspapers had campaigned against supposed Jewish crimes.

By far the largest contingent of immigrants had crossed the

border from Canada, and half of the Canadians had been born in Quebec, where there had been a surge of ritual murder talk in the first three decades of the twentieth century. For most of the European immigrants, the blood libel likely existed as subconscious social knowledge; for the Québécois, linked to their home province by geographical proximity and family ties, the intense antisemitic agitation of Quebec City and Montreal belonged to their everyday lives. Did members of Massena's French-Canadian community launch the ritual murder accusation in the wake of Barbara Griffiths's disappearance?

Unfortunately, we know little about the social and political views of members of Massena's large immigrant population. As noncitizens, they didn't have the right to vote, so we can't use electoral tallies to glean political affiliations. But if their ideas, attitudes, and inclinations can't be known, we do have specific information about many of them, thanks to a remarkable historical source: the records of Alcoa's "Twenty-Five Year Service Club," which commemorate the lives and careers of every worker who reached his (and, occasionally, her) twenty-fifth anniversary with the company.[1]

Alcoa began in 1888 as the Pittsburgh Reduction Company. The word "reduction" referred to the complex process of reducing away the impurities of "alumina," a natural metal, to produce pure aluminum. Alumina is an abundant ore that makes up about 8 percent of the Earth's crust and exists in virtually all common rocks. The problem for the chemists who discovered alumina in the late eighteenth century was the extreme difficulty of extracting, or smelting, it from the other substances to which it is tightly bonded in nature. Alumina, by itself, is largely useless; aluminum is one of the great building materials of the modern world.[2]

Inventors began experimenting with the smelting of aluminum in the early nineteenth century, but it wasn't until the 1850s that anyone succeeded in producing a significant quantity of the pure metal. The amount of energy required to extract aluminum from its impunities, however, made the process prohibitively expensive—about $500 a pound, or more than twice the price of platinum or gold.[3] At this stage, aluminum counted as a "precious metal" rather than as one that entrepreneurs could put to industrial use.

By 1860, scientists from various countries had succeeded in reducing the cost of pure aluminum to $17 a pound, the same price as silver, but this was still too high. Finally, in 1886, the American chemist Charles Martin Hall figured out how to extract aluminum from its ore using cryolite, a powerful chemical solvent, heated to 1,012°C. Hall heated the solvent by applying direct electric current (electrolysis) to the mixture of alumina and cryolite. The cryolite, now in molten form, dissolved the alumina into its different chemical elements, allowing Hall to extract the pure aluminum.[4]

The process required a vast amount of electricity, which until the 1880s could be produced only by batteries that were expensive to make and usable only once or twice. But engineers had recently invented turbines powered by coal and natural gas, both plentiful in many parts of the United States, and this new way of producing electricity dramatically reduced its cost and, in turn, the cost of smelting aluminum. The smelting process was now cheap enough—$4 a pound in 1889—to permit the mass production of aluminum.[5]

Hall applied to patent his new procedure—cryolite plus turbine-produced electrolysis—only to find that a French inventor, Paul L. T. Héroult, had come up with a similar process at about the same time. Héroult also applied for a patent, but the American courts ruled, probably incorrectly, that Hall had filed his claim first. It would make him a wealthy man.[6] Armed with his patent, Hall and several backers, including the banker and investor Andrew W. Mellon, established the Pittsburgh Reduction Company to smelt aluminum on an industrial scale. They centered their smelting operation around a huge chamber packed with rectangular vats, which Hall called "pots." Each pot contained a precise amount of alumina and cryolite, plus a cathode (negative pole) and anode (positive pole) for applying electric current. As the current flowed into each pot, Hall's workers harvested large amounts of pure aluminum. Linked together, this collection of pots formed a "potroom," overseen by skilled workers known as "potmen."

The cost of aluminum smelting declined even more when the company opened plants in Niagara Falls and Massena, where harnessed water power created a limitless supply of cheap electricity. Aluminum-making became still more efficient after 1910, when officials of the Pittsburgh Reduction Company, renamed Alcoa in 1907, realized that bauxite, a rock made of clay, contained a higher concentration of alumina—50 percent—than any other rock. Bauxite became the ore of choice, especially after Alcoa adopted the Bayer process, a method of extracting alumina invented in 1905 by the Austrian chemist Karl Josef Bayer.[7] Alcoa then bought as many bauxite mines as it could find, allowing the company, in successive steps, to mine the

The potroom at the Massena plant, c. 1910

rock, extract the alumina, and smelt large quantities of pure aluminum. By the early 1900s, aluminum had become one of the world's great industrial products; its light weight, malleability, and durability would make it ideal for bicycle frames, pots and pans, beverage containers, auto parts, skis, outdoor furniture, and countless other things.

Aluminum also transformed Massena into an industrial town and made it a mecca for immigrants seeking a new life in the United States. Tony Macre, who emigrated as a young man from Italy, became the first member of Alcoa's Twenty-Five Year Service Club in 1931, having arrived in upstate New York in 1905. Like many immigrants who landed in Massena, Macre attended the town's Americanization School, going to evening class after a full day of work. During his studies, the other students made him "flag-bearer" for the school.[8]

Another early member of the club was Simon Smucz, born in Szatmár County in eastern Hungary in 1890. Smucz emigrated to the United States alone as a fifteen-year-old boy, traveling directly to Massena, where he had relatives. He found a job as an unskilled worker at Alcoa four years later and, after twenty-three years, worked his way up to head potman.[9]

Like Smucz, Dominick Attilio Pellegrino emigrated to the United States as a young boy, just thirteen years old. His hometown was Cerisano, Italy, and on arriving in Massena in 1901, he took a job as a water boy at one of the canals under construction. After a summer of work, he had saved enough to buy his first American clothes and to repay his father for the voyage to America. His work for Alcoa was initially menial: water boy, errand boy, and groundskeeper. He returned to Italy in 1907 for his required military service—suggesting that he didn't plan to remain in the United States. Nonetheless, he came back to Massena and worked this time on Alcoa's loading dock. In 1912, at the age of twenty-four, he traveled to Italy once again, to marry his childhood sweetheart. Alcoa had given him a six-month leave and, back at the company in 1913, he became foreman of the loading yard. We lose track of him for the next twenty-odd years but learn that in 1935, he would vacation with his elderly parents in the Italian village of his birth.[10]

Joseph Mittiga of Plati, Italy, didn't return home as often as Pellegrino, but after working on the Massena power canal from 1898 to 1902, he too sailed back to Italy to find a bride. Mittiga stayed in his hometown for five years before returning to Massena. He took a job at Alcoa and worked there continuously for thirty-six years.[11] Joseph's brother Michael also emigrated from Plati, leaving his life as a farmer in 1900. In Massena, Michael landed a job in construction and remained for five years before heading back to Italy to marry. He remigrated to Massena in 1906, a year before his brother's return to the upstate village, and began his decades-long career at Alcoa, mostly as an unskilled laborer.

Rocco Trimboli, also of Plati, Italy, followed a similar path, although starting later in life. Born in 1866, he came to Massena at age thirty-one, already married, and found work as a laborer on Massena's power canal. After five years in Massena, he left for Italy and didn't resume his American life until 1907. At Alcoa, he worked in construction and later in the cable mill.[12] We often think of immigrants as remaining in the United States permanently, but like Pellegrino, the Mittiga brothers, and Trimboli, many returned regularly to their home countries and maintained ties with family there. They also reconnected with their home cultures, which, in the case of Italy, likely exposed them to antisemitism and the ritual murder charge. About a third of those who emigrated to the United States returned at some point to their native lands and stayed there, perhaps now with enough money to buy property and start a family.[13]

Once people emigrated from one town or region, others followed in their wake to the same places in the United States. Massena fit this pattern perfectly, as certain European towns and villages were overrepresented among the immigrants who settled there. Plati, Italy, an impoverished, Mafia-ridden village of some 5,000 souls in 1920, may have topped the list—at least among members of Alcoa's Twenty-Five Year Service Club. Like Trimboli and the Mittiga brothers, Sam Triccase emigrated from Plati to Massena, where he found a job in the Alcoa plant and spent his career doing unskilled labor.[14] Yet another former Plati resident was Salvatore LaRosa, who arrived in Massena in 1922 and worked in Alcoa's rodding and resmelting departments.[15]

Beyond Italy, the countries of origin best represented among the Alcoa workers with twenty-five-year-long careers were Hungary, Canada (both Ontario and Quebec), Poland, Spain, and Portugal. This Twenty-Five Year Service Club sample understates the number of Canadians employed at the aluminum company because they were less likely than the European immigrants to remain with the firm continuously for decades. The Canadians' families were close by, and they could easily recross the border if and when opportunities seemed better in their home country. In the early part of the twentieth century, white people—Chinese were another story—could traverse the border between the United States and Canada almost at will. (As a child in the 1960s, I remember car trips across the border to Cornwall, Ontario; my parents didn't have to show any ID.) French speakers were more likely to stay in the United States than English speakers, since French Canadians were generally treated as second-class citizens at home.[16]

It's notable that in the first four decades of the twentieth century, immigrants could work for many years at companies like Alcoa without being U.S. citizens or obtaining work or residence permits (green cards). John Wasylec, for example, a native of Wotostkow, Poland, emigrated to the United States in 1913 at age nineteen. He didn't become a citizen until 1931, having worked at Alcoa for sixteen years.[17] It took twenty years for Janos Czerlan, originally from Hungary, to gain U.S. citizenship, and twenty-one years for Michael Keerd, of Finnish origin, to become a naturalized American.[18]

Keerd's story is especially interesting. He became a seaman at age fifteen and, after plying the Baltic, found his way onto a

British ship bound for New York. While on shore leave, Keerd saw a sign advertising employment in "an aluminum plant" in Massena and hopped on a train. His first impressions of Massena and Alcoa were negative: the town was too cold and the potrooms too hot. He planned to head back to sea but then "made a few friends" and decided to stay. Over the years, he worked his way up to head potman and then foreman. He married a Canadian woman, with whom he had four children, and one joined him at Alcoa. His other son enlisted in the army, and his two daughters found work close by as a store clerk and a nurse. During the Second World War, Keerd lost touch with his family in Finland and never saw them again.[19]

As for French-speaking Canadians, the Twenty-Five Year Service Club included Albert Degagne, a native of St. Pamphile, Quebec, who worked as a carbon changer in the potroom. Michel Bouchard had made the short fifty-mile journey from Ormstown, Quebec, to Massena, where he served as an ingot controlman in Alcoa's resmelting department. Jacques Cousineau had come from Montcerf, Quebec, arriving in Massena in 1923 and becoming a U.S. citizen fifteen years later. Cousineau worked as a lathe operator.[20]

Cousineau's fifteen-year wait for naturalization appears to be about the average for members of the Service Club, although several faced a twenty- to thirty-year delay. The shortest path to citizenship of any foreign-born member of the Twenty-Five Year Service Club was eleven years. The ability to work without having residence permits or citizenship papers stemmed from the vast need for workers in a rapidly industrializing United States. In Massena, it may also have had to do with an unwillingness to hire African Americans. Not a single member of the Service Club was African American—each dossier included a photograph—and as a consequence, the black population of Massena was vanishingly small: just twenty-seven persons or about two-tenths of one percent.[21] Perhaps African Americans were uninterested in an isolated town such as Massena, but this seems unlikely, given the massive black migration of the early twentieth century from the South to the North. In part, African Americans were fleeing Jim Crow, but even more important was the lure of steady industrial jobs.[22]

It wasn't just European and Canadian immigrants who worked at Alcoa; plenty of U.S.-born people did as well. But the Twenty-Five Year Service Club included almost twice as many immigrants as native-born, at least for the years 1902 to 1928.[23] U.S. citizens enjoyed more opportunities than immigrants and didn't have to remain with a single employer for twenty-five years. In any case, native-born Americans mostly held the higher-paying jobs at Alcoa; immigrants were rarely promoted to shop foreman or to white-collar positions.

Harold Phelps, American-born, began his career with Alcoa in 1915. After returning from the war, he worked as a machinist, rising by 1931 to shop foreman with a middle-class income. The Service Club's records list earnings only for the last five years before an employee's twenty-fifth anniversary with the firm—in Phelps's case, 1939–44. During the war years, when aluminum was hotly in demand and labor was scarce, workers were paid considerably more than during the Great Depression. Phelps remained at the plant throughout the Second World War, earning his peak annual salary of $3,380.87 in 1942, which today would have a buying power of about $49,000.[24] Alexander Ori, a native of Hungary, came to Alcoa in 1918 and worked mainly as a laborer or janitor. His best year was 1943, when he made $2,394.38, or about $34,000 in today's dollars and 30 percent less than Phelps's pay.

We don't know what Ori earned in the 1930s, but another laborer, Steve Szpak, originally from Poland, made $1,049.69 in 1936 and $1,442.04 three years later. In today's dollars, his earnings would have been about $18,500 and $25,400 for the two respective years. John Kish, a Hungary native, worked in the potroom as a carbon changer, a job that required some skill, and he did somewhat better than a simple laborer: $1,414.66 in 1936 and $2,040.96 in 1939. Today's equivalents would be $25,000 and $36,000. Pay was consistent within the different categories of work, so these figures are representative of what others earned. The salary difference between 1936 and 1939 had to do with the economic upswing of the decade's end, when workers were less likely to be furloughed or laid off than they had been three years earlier.

Edward Serra, originally of Portugal, ranked among the highest-paid former immigrants in the Service Club's records. Having worked as a nurse in a hospital, he would have been better educated than the typical immigrant, a teenage boy with only a few years of formal schooling. Serra became an assistant foreman and foreman in the 1930s, earning $2,766.06 in 1937 ($47,000 today) and $2,834 in 1939 (almost $50,000 today). Compare Serra with Frank Robillard, a Massena native, who became a general foreman in the late 1930s and, as *Alcoa News* put it, "one of the most prominent leaders of the community," serving as a member of the Massena Village Board.[25] Robillard earned $3,380 in 1938 ($59,000 today) and $3,470 in 1940 ($61,000 today).

These records show that a foreman earned twice as much as

a laborer in 1939, but even the laborer made more per week than the average industrial worker nationwide. Alcoa laborers earned $1,400–$1,500 per year, while the average person employed in manufacturing made $1,300.[26] The Massena advantage was in large part the result of seniority: the Alcoa workers for whom we have wage data had been employed there for at least twenty years.

As for the more skilled occupations, such as carbon changer in a potroom, Alcoa's Massena workers also did better than the national average. John Kish earned $2,041 in 1939, while his counterpart nationally made $1,529.[27] For all aluminum workers nationwide, average annual earnings amounted to $1,433 in 1939, still worse than the average for that year of Alcoa's Massena workers with twenty or more years of seniority.[28]

All in all, these Alcoa wages were modest, but they stood at the national average or better and, judging from the considerable number of twenty-five-year veterans, seemed to offer the opportunity for steady work. There was, however, a clear inequality between native- and foreign-born workers, and that inequality might have been a source of resentment, a resentment that could have spilled over onto Massena's Jewish shopkeepers. Wages are meaningful only in relation to prices, and if the Jews were deemed to charge too much for their goods—as European antisemites commonly alleged at this time—the Jews might have been seen as exploiters.

But who exactly were the Jews of Massena?[29] The original membership list of the synagogue founded in 1919 shows thirty-four names, including more than one member of the same family and five from neighboring towns. So Massena housed about twenty-five Jewish families at the time Congregation Adath Israel (Community of Israel) was incorporated. One of the

Ida and Jesse Kauffman, 1898

founders was my great-grandfather Jesse J. Kauffman, who had come to Massena in 1898. A photograph taken that year shows Jesse seated with my grandmother Hattie perched on his lap.

My great-grandmother Ida stands next to him with her hand resting on Hattie's head. Ida looks elegant in her floor-length dress, with its pinched waist, tight arm-length sleeves, padded shoulders, and flared collar reaching almost to her ears. Her light hair has been pulled back tightly to emphasize the regular features of her face. Jesse wears a long dark coat with contrasting trousers, a vest, and high, starched collar. His mustache points downward in an inverted V, and his dark curly hair has been combed back to reveal a high forehead and a small widow's peak.[30]

Like a great many Jewish immigrant men, Jesse began his career as a peddler. Ida, meanwhile, gained valuable experience managing her family's store. Together they opened a small shop in Massena and then a larger one, which they rented for $15 a month. The couple lived in a small apartment above the shop. During its first decade and a half, the Kauffmans' store fronted an unpaved, unlighted street. Transactions were made in cash, and the business struggled. Still, their modest earnings didn't prevent them from expanding the family: their son Abe was born in 1900. Jesse became a U.S. citizen that same year.

Abe graduated from Massena High School as valedictorian in 1918 and enrolled at Cornell University, completing his degree four years later. He moved briefly to New York City but

Kauffman's Department Store, 1908

returned to Massena to help manage the family business. His sisters Hattie, Sadie, and Anne all finished college or university, an accomplishment unusual for women at the time. Hattie joined the family business, Sadie became an elementary school teacher, and Anne was an actress before marrying a psychiatrist and settling in New York City. Sadie remained unmarried; Hattie wed my grandfather in March 1919, giving birth to my father the following December. Abe didn't marry until after the Second World War at age forty-six.

Sometime in the late 1920s, Jesse traveled to his hometown in what was then Germany, now Poland. On the way, he stopped in Paris where he collected samples from major fashion houses, saying he'd order the clothing lines once back in New York—he didn't specify that it was *Massena*, New York, rather than New York City. Arriving in Bielica, Jesse turned the samples into gifts and gave them to his grateful relatives. The American's real gift was to buy a ticket to New York for his cousin Rachel and bring her home with him. Rachel turned out to be the lone member of her immediate family to survive the Holocaust.[31]

Jesse's son-in-law, my grandfather Edward Berenson, was the first of the extended Kauffman family to pass away, dying in 1935 after undergoing surgery in a New York City hospital. He was just forty-one. Obituaries leave the cause of his early death unclear, although one said he died after having his tonsils and adenoids removed.[32] Family lore has it that he died from cancer, his life something of a disappointment because antisemitism, it was said, prevented him from finding an engineering job in Boston, his hometown. Jesse died in 1950 and Ida three years later. Abe ran the Kauffman store, the oldest in St. Lawrence County.[33]

Massena's far more successful store belonged to the Levine family, founded by the twenty-nine-year-old Sam Levine in 1907. Sam had come to the United States from the village of Dokshitz in what was then Polish territory. He left home at age seventeen, with stays in Koenigsberg, Huss, England, Quebec City, and Montreal, before arriving in Tupper Lake, New York, after a two-year-long journey. He became a peddler and trooped around upstate New York selling clothes. Sam would marry into a family that had arrived in the United States from western Russia via South Africa, where his father-in-law-to-be, Chaim Friedlander, accumulated the money to move with his entire family to the United States. In Tupper Lake—so the story goes—Chaim saw Sam as good husband material for his two daughters and told Sam to choose one or the other. He picked Lena, and two weeks later they married—without so much as kissing beforehand.

They had six children, all of whom worked after school and during the summer alongside their mother and father in the store. Massena's Jewish women played key roles in their families' businesses and juggled child raising with their commercial responsibilities, often by hiring young Jewish women to help at home. The eldest of the Levine children took over the business rather than enroll in college and made it into a highly successful concern. The other children also worked in the store, even after attending top universities. The one exception was Abe, the third child, who became a physician and opened a practice in Massena. The lure of Massena and family remained strong: children who had gone away to college and spent time in New York City almost always returned to Massena.[34] This pattern would repeat itself until at least the third generation.

A photograph from 1940 shows Sam Levine with his daughter Alice standing in front of the family store. With his wide, broad mustache, Sam resembles Groucho Marx; Alice, in heels, towers over him.

The large Levine family was intertwined with the Rossoff family, connected as they were by marriage in several different generations. Such connections were common among Massena's Jews; since the number of Jewish families in the area remained small, Jews selected marriage partners from a narrow pool.

When Alex Rossoff emigrated from Russia to the United States in 1906 at age seventeen, Massena beckoned because he had several relatives there. His cousin Sam Levine employed Alex in his store, and before long, the young Rossoff opened his own establishment. Alex's sister Rebecca came to the United States a year after he did and, at first, stayed in New York City working in the sweatshops of the garment industry. On a visit to her brother in Massena, she met the Levines and the Kauffmans and worked in the homes of both families. Their other brother Meyer eventually landed in Massena and found a job in Alex's store. In 1918, Rebecca married Nathan Jacobs, who had come to Massena two years earlier after seeing a *New York Times* advertisement seeking workers at Alcoa. Jacobs lasted at the factory less than three days, repelled by the harsh working conditions. To support himself, he turned to peddling and later to the "junk" business, which meant selling scrap metal, rags, bottles, tires, chickens, and almost anything else in demand. Nathan and Rebecca's son Sam, nicknamed Jackie, eventually took over the family business even though he had graduated first in his class at Syracuse University and earned a law degree from Yale. Jackie Jacobs and my father, both born in 1919, became best friends and remained close until my father married and eventually left Massena in 1951. Jackie was a fine writer, and he made notable contributions to the history of Massena, penning a sharp critique of Saul Friedman's 1978 book about the Massena blood libel.[35] Massena's two most prominent Jewish families were the Slavins and the Shulkins, long allied as business partners. Sam Slavin's immigration story resembles those of the other Jews who ended up in Massena. As for Jake Shulkin, his personal history is more colorful. At age twenty, Jake had been conscripted into the Russian army, a fate that promised years of hardship, or worse. To rescue him, two of his sisters devised an audacious plan. Posing as prostitutes, they drove a horse-drawn wagon into the fortified military compound where Jake's unit was confined. They dressed Jake in women's clothing, hid him in their wagon under a thick layer of straw, and spirited him away. Now AWOL, Jake remained in hiding until his family arranged for his passage to the United States. He was already engaged to be married and convinced his fiancée to give him her dowry on the understanding that, once settled in America, he would send for her.

Jake took a slow boat across the North Atlantic to Quebec and then traveled by train to Buffalo and then to New York City. He found work there as a tailor and fell in love with his first cousin, Sarah Saidel, who had also emigrated from Polish Russia. He wrote his fiancée asking to be released from his marriage commitment. She responded, as the story goes, by hexing him and his family. Jake and Sarah married in 1907 and quickly had three children. In an effort to improve his fortunes, he opened a newspaper and candy stand in a subway station. But the damp, underground air seemed to threaten his already fragile health. Sarah, too, was ailing in New York City, as were their three children, who seemed at risk for tuberculosis.

A doctor advised them to flee to the country, and since they had relatives upstate, they made their way to Massena, whose frigid wintertime temperatures and humid summers made it a less than ideal choice. But once established in Massena, they produced two more children, and Jake's partnership with Sam Slavin prospered. Jake became president of Congregation Adath Israel and would represent it during the traumatic blood libel to come.

So, of course, would the rabbi, Berel Brennglass, who was also advised to move upstate from New York City for medical reasons. In his case the rationale was more compelling. The rabbi's brother, a medical doctor, diagnosed him with tuberculosis in 1915 and sent him for treatment to the renowned TB clinic in Saranac Lake, a resort town in the northern Adirondacks. Brennglass settled in nearby Tupper Lake, where the small Jewish community hired him as their rabbi. He had come to the United States alone, leaving his wife and four children in Cardiff, Wales, his stopping point for about a decade and a half after fleeing his native Lithuania together with his wife's family in 1900.[36] Brennglass had studied at the yeshiva in Kovmo, Lithuania, and was ordained as a rabbi around 1900. It's unclear whether he headed a congregation in Lithuania, but in Cardiff he didn't, working as a peddler alongside his wife's relatives. In this profession, the scholarly 5-foot, 2-inch man failed miserably, but for reasons unknown he did not find a position in a local synagogue.

Berel Brennglass, alone among his male siblings, attended no secular schools. His three sisters, all older than he, learned to read and write but do not seem to have worked outside the home. Two sisters, Goldie and Rebecca, emigrated to the United States; the third, Sora, remained in Lithuania. The oldest of his four brothers, Abram, became a physician and never left Lithuania. Another brother Khaim, died shortly after birth, and the other two, Joachim and Solomon, moved to America in the 1890s. In Lithuania, Joachim graduated from a gymnasium (academic high school) and university, where he became a revolutionary. His anti-tsarist activities landed him in prison, and immediately after being released, he sailed to New York. Joachim enrolled in pharmacy school and then Columbia University medical school, eventually becoming a successful pediatrician. Solomon, eleven years younger than Joachim, became a pharmacist and settled in Manhattan. Neither of the two men was religious, although they raised their children as Jews.[37]

In 1907, Berel sailed to New York to visit his siblings but returned to Cardiff after only a short stay in the United States. Did he plan to emigrate and then change his mind? Was there a family emergency that drew him back to Wales? Berel's grandson didn't know, although he said that his grandfather regretted the lack of a secular education, doubting perhaps that he could find a suitable professional job in New York, as his brothers had.[38] In any case, Berel spent another eight years in Cardiff.

He returned alone to New York in 1915 and landed his first position as a rabbi in Tupper Lake two years later. Again, he set sail for Wales, this time to fetch his family and lead them to upstate New York. This was his third round-trip between Cardiff and New York since 1900, an uncommon amount of travel for Jewish immigrants to the United States, most of whom never returned to Europe.

Massena's new Congregation Adath Israel snatched Berel Brennglass from Tupper Lake with an offer of $23 a week plus a house within a short walking distance of the synagogue. His annual salary of $1,196 plus his free rent and earnings from blessing kosher meat made his total income comparable to that of an unskilled laborer at Alcoa. The family was poor and lived modestly, the children wearing hand-me-downs and delivering newspapers to make a bit of cash. But Brennglass enjoyed a clergyman's prestige and became one of Massena's best-known residents. He was unimpressed with his congregants' knowledge of Jewish ritual and the Hebrew Bible but didn't press them to be more orthodox. His grandson called him an "accommodationist" who appreciated whatever small gains in Jewish understanding and observance he could evoke. For him, just two families, the Jacobs and the Shulkins, counted as genuine Orthodox Jews.[39]

Although Rabbi Brennglass's back-and-forth travel between Cardiff and New York made him stand apart from the rest of Massena's Jews, in most other ways his personal history resembled theirs. They had come from the same part of Europe as he, the men by themselves, the women with brothers or their entire family. Several of the men had left the Russian Empire to escape military conscription. Rebecca Landsman, among other women, told of becoming exasperated with antisemitic insults and discrimination and of their desire to escape to the land of the free.

Arriving in New York, often by circuitous routes, Jews made their way upstate to Massena because they had relatives there or close by and heard that opportunities existed in the industrializing town. The men typically began as peddlers and then opened stores. With but few exceptions, they didn't work at Alcoa. My grandfather was one of those exceptions, but as a chemical engineer, he had a professional job rather than an assignment on the factory floor. Even so, he left Alcoa after just two years. Like most Massena Jews, Edward Berenson wanted the relative independence of his own, or a family, business.

As for Massena's Jewish women, some already had shopkeeping experience before getting married, and even if they didn't, they quickly learned the retail business. Most women worked in their husbands' shops, but some Massena women went into business for themselves. Rebecca Landsman, who married Louis Clopman, a junk and scrap-metal dealer, bought her brother's rooming house and grocery store as part of an arrangement that enabled him to buy a meat market. Rose Kauffman, Abe's wife, tired of working in her husband's store and opened a shop of her own.

If most of Massena's Jews didn't become prosperous, they earned acceptable livings, enough to raise families, often large ones with four, five, or six children.[40] They were thankful to be in the United States rather than Russia and although they heard anti-Jewish epithets from time to time, they complained little of hostility to Jews.

The situation for Jews could not have been more different across the St. Lawrence River in Quebec, where they faced a fierce, European-style antisemitism in the first decades of the twentieth century. Some of this anti-Jewish hatred came from the strong influence in Quebec of France's Edouard Drumont, whom one historian called "the most popular modern anti-Jewish polemicist before Adolf Hitler."[41] Drumont's best-selling book, *Judaized France*, had expressed a new racialized form of antisemitism that appealed to working people and shopkeepers harmed by the Long Depression of the late nineteenth century and also to traditionalist elements in the Catholic Church. These views took hold in Quebec after 1900 as part of a French-Canadian reaction to the immigration of Eastern European Jews to their province. A mounting Quebecois nationalism saw Jews as representing a dangerous, alien culture, a culture that threatened to undermine the religiosity of the province's overwhelmingly Catholic population.[42]

Quebec's Catholic establishment tended to be traditionalist— "ultramontane" or "devoted to the pope," as religious leaders put it. And as in Europe of the late nineteenth century, ultramontane Catholics ranked among the main proponents of antisemitism. In 1908, the Catholic Association of Canadian Youth created a militant antisemitic league modeled on Europe's increasingly popular anti-Jewish movements. The association placed "the Jewish question" front and center, as did a new antisemitic newspaper, *Catholic Social Action*, and a series of tracts, almanacs, manuals, and books spawned by the paper.[43] Quebec's City's small Jewish community—275 people in 1900 in an overall population of nearly 55,000—responded by forming a civil rights organization, but it was powerless in the face of a campaign against them by leaders of the Catholic Church.[44]

Those leaders organized a series of anti-Jewish lectures in which one speaker, L. C. Farley, urged his audience "to drive the Jew politely far out of Canada and particularly from Quebec." What proved to be the most consequential speech in the series came from a prominent Catholic notary, Jacques-Édouard

Plamondon, a disciple of Drumont's who founded a newspaper with the same title as his, *La libre parole* (Free Speech). Entitled simply "The Jew," Plamondon's speech baldly stated that the Jew was "a thief of our property, a corrupter of our women, and the murderer of Christian children."[45] The fact that there had been so many recent ritual murder trials in Europe, Plamondon added, proved the "undeniable authenticity" of the charge. The notary also claimed the Talmud required Jews to lie, cheat, and steal and declared that "the Jews of Poland and of Russia . . . destroy the populations of entire villages with poisoned whiskey."[46] In general, Plamondon said, the Jews threatened "the purity and sacredness of Quebec's rural way of life" and would eventually destroy that life, just as they had done in Europe.[47]

Although Quebec's Protestants, mostly of British heritage, showed more hostility to Catholics than to Jews, they didn't dispute Plamondon's premises. "We do not admit that the Jews are a lovable race," declared the editors of the *Chronicle*, Quebec's leading Protestant paper, "their racial characteristics are too strongly defined for that."[48] Quebec's Catholics and Protestants were united in seeing Jews as a "race" and usually an alien one at that. But Protestants generally didn't join Catholics in trying to make antisemitism the foundation of a political movement.

After Plamondon's speech, Quebec's Jews found themselves under threat. To supposedly discourage Jews from murdering Christian children, young Catholic men assaulted Jews on the street; vandalized their homes, shops, and synagogues; and abused them verbally, especially with the ritual murder accusation. Plamondon urged his followers to boycott Jewish stores and to stop selling them houses to prevent more Jews from settling in Quebec.

It was the ritual murder accusation, and the potential dangers it represented to Quebec's Jewish community, that moved two of the province's most prominent Jews, Benjamin Ortenberg and Louis Lazarovitch, to sue Plamondon for libel. They argued that Plamondon had made dangerous, false claims against them as individuals and against Quebec's Jews as a group. Ortenberg and Lazarovitch also maintained that Plamondon had threatened them physically and harmed their livelihoods by organizing a boycott of their businesses.[49] The case, including appeals, extended over nearly four years, from 1910 to 1914.

It was a difficult case to make. Canadian law didn't recognize the defamation of a group, only individuals, and Plamondon maintained not only that his statements were truthful, rather than libelous, but also that he had directed them against all Jews, wherever they lived, and not against Ortenberg and Lazarovitch, whom he didn't know personally. In essence, the lawsuit called for the courts to punish what we would today call "hate speech," a category that didn't yet exist in Canadian law. The two plaintiffs asked for only minimal damages, $500; a larger amount would have required a jury trial, which the Jews knew would go against them, given the widespread hostility they faced in Quebec.

As most observers expected, the judge ruled against Ortenberg and Lazarovitch. "The defendant," he declared, "incriminates only the Jewish race, its doctrines, and its religious and social practices without attacking the plaintiff in particular." The plaintiff, therefore, "being neither named nor specially indicated, has no recourse civilly against the defendant."[50] The court, in other words, did not rule on the truth or falsity of Plamondon's accusation of ritual murder; it said only that no Canadian law had been violated.

The plaintiff's attorney, Samuel W. Jacob, had always planned to appeal, and in the higher court he prevailed. The appellate judge ruled that Quebec City's Jewish population was so small—just 75 households—that Plamondon did, in fact, know its members personally, which meant that his attacks were directed against individuals. Since his statements were false, they violated Canadian law. The fines imposed were minimal, just $75, a sum so paltry that Plamondon claimed he had been vindicated. And besides, the court had condemned only his statements against Ortenberg and Lazarovitch, not his criticism of Jews in general.

Although Quebec's Jews won in the end, it was a pyrrhic victory. The trial had enabled Plamondon to use the forum of the court, as well as the case's elaborate coverage in the press, to gain wide publicity for his tirades against the Jews. When accused of defaming Jewish citizens, Plamondon responded that everything he had said was true. He added that the Jews, "having come in large numbers to Canada . . . have become a social scourge . . . to the imminent danger of the Christian people, and of the Christian institutions of this province."[51] The three prominent priests who testified on Plamondon's behalf reinforced his position by asserting, falsely, that Roman Catholic literature confirmed the reality of Jewish ritual murder, as did a huge amount of supposedly scholarly work. In response, Ortenberg and Lazarovitch's attorney could say only that the scholarship they had cited during the trial was more reliable than what the priests had presented. The problem was that the average Quebecois newspaper reader had no ability to evaluate the conflicting "scholarly" claims; for the most part, they believed what their side had to say. Tragically for Quebec's Jews, the legal process they had set in motion forced them to participate in an argument about whether Jewish ritual murder was real. This argument doubtless convinced many Quebecois that Plamondon was right.

In the aftermath of the case, a host of Quebec antisemites went on the offensive. They claimed that the Jews had prevailed in court, both in Quebec and in Kiev—the Beilis case took place simultaneously with the Plamondon one—only because they controlled the international press and because their money had allowed them to purchase the best lawyers dollars could buy. For Father Antonio Huot, editor of the Drumont-influenced ultramontane paper, the *Quebec Religious Weekly*, the Jewish victories in court didn't make ritual murder untrue. This Jewish crime was, rather, "a fact duly recorded by history," and Quebec's Catholics had to protect their families from the danger that Jews would kidnap and kill their children.[52] Huot was more a yellow journalist than a respected clergyman, but Monsignor Louis-Adolphe Paquet, an important figure in the Quebec Church, expressed similar ideas. In his multivolume *The Public Law of the Church* (1908–15), he wrote, "The Jew, for us, is an enemy [whose] influence penetrates and dominates any Catholic people or group [and] threatens them as well."[53] Although the suit against Plamondon created sympathy for Quebec's Jews in parts of English-speaking Canada, in Quebec it likely made antisemitism worse.

In the 1920s, Montreal, now a sizable city, became the center of new ritual murder accusations. During the teens, Eastern European Jews had flooded into the city, and by 1921 they represented 6.1 percent of the population.[54] French Canadian nationalists and ultramontanists in the Church denounced the Jewish immigrants for taking jobs away from real Quebecois and for undercutting Catholic shopkeepers with their peddlers' carts. The wealthier Jews, it was said, embodied the dangers of international capitalism, while the poorer ones, some of them socialists and communists, had brought the menace of Bolshevism to Montreal. To make matters worse, in the view of Quebec's nationalists, Jewish immigrants sent their children to Protestant schools, where they learned English, not French, and linked their fortunes to the Protestant minority that dominated the economy and kept Catholics in their place.[55]

In the 1920s, a variety of journalists and traditionalist Catholics regularly voiced the ritual murder accusation and referred approvingly to the notorious anti-Jewish forgery, *The Protocols of the Elders of Zion*, which Henry Ford had publicized in the United States. Toward the end of the decade, two new French-language antisemitic newspapers, *Le Miroir* and *Le Goglu*, announced that "Jews are murderers" and called for boycotts of Jewish stores. A few years later, in a banner, front-page headline, *Le Miroir* called Jews "drinkers of blood." The article beneath, paraphrasing a "report" by the Nazi propagandist Alfred Rosenberg, declared that in Russia, "the Jews had slit the throats of 40 million Christians in less than five years. . . . This is what we can expect from Jewish domination in every country of the world—barbarism that exceeds the barbarism of cannibals."[56] In a subsequent issue, *Le Miroir* ran a cartoon showing a rabbi slitting the throat of Simon of Trent, the famous "victim" of the archetypal ritual murder case of 1475.[57]

These newspapers, together with religious organizations like the Catholic Association of Canadian Youth, militant leagues, and various propaganda organs, gave Quebec a genuine antisemitic movement, with ties to its European counterparts and considerable popular support. The United States would never develop such a movement, despite a fair amount of antisemitic propaganda in the 1920s and 1930s. The absence of organized antisemitism in America helped make its Jewish population more secure than anywhere else, although American Jews would suffer discrimination, ugly stereotyping, and a variety of other indignities. This peculiarly American form of Jew-hatred provides yet another frame for understanding the Massena case.

Le Miroir, Montreal

Chapter 4

THE MASSENA CASE AND AMERICAN ANTISEMITISM

Elderly Massena Jews alive at the time of the ritual murder accusation or born shortly afterwards had deep-seated memories of hostility to Jews. Doris Robinson revealed that schoolmates routinely called her a "Christ-killer" and said that while she was walking picket lines during Alcoa strikes, anti-union people smeared her with a variety of anti-Jewish epithets.[1] Alice Rosen, at the age of 102, recalled her belief that there would be a pogrom at the time of the blood libel. She and her Jewish friends stayed indoors as much as possible. Rosen also remembered having "Christ-killer" hurled at her on the way to school.[2]

Most of the Gentiles I interviewed in 2015 and 2016 knew little or nothing of the blood libel, even though it had received some publicity a few years earlier when Shirley Vernick published a work of children's fiction based on the case.[3] Massena's

Jews all knew something about it. Alan Brennglass, the rabbi's grandson, grew up with the story, hearing constantly about it, not from Berel, who wanted to put its traumatic memory behind him, but from his parents. His mother hoped to bring it to the attention of the American public in the 1950s by writing a teleplay about the incident.[4] No network appears to have been interested. After the Holocaust, the Massena blood libel seemed perhaps a small matter, and in any case, most Americans liked to see themselves as largely immune from antisemitism. They weren't, of course, but relative to most European countries—and to Canada—hatred of Jews in the United States was mild.

During the first century or so of American history, Jews enjoyed a perhaps unprecedented degree of security and well-being. Until the late nineteenth century, their numbers were minuscule and, given the vastness of the United States, most Americans didn't notice them. In 1776, the United States's 1,000 Jews represented less than one tenth of one percent of the population. In 1840, there were just 15,000 Jews in the entire country, and in 1880, as the massive Jewish emigration from Eastern Europe was getting underway, the United States counted 250,000 Jews or still only one-half of one percent.[5]

Although in European countries even tiny numbers of Jews could appear threatening to Christians, the upsurge of antisemitic hostility in the Old World corresponded to what Albert S. Lindemann calls "the rise of the Jews"—the rapid nineteenth-century increase in the number of Jews relative to the population at large.[6] In the United States, this relative increase was smaller than in most Eastern European countries, and it occurred in a context of unusual, perhaps unprecedented religious toleration.

The U.S. Constitution invested ultimate authority not in God, but in "We the People," and the First Amendment provided that "Congress shall make no law respecting an establishment of religion, or prohibiting the free exercise thereof."[7] This amendment did not, of course, resolve all questions about the relationship of church and state, but it prevented one religion from being formally superior at the national level to others, as the Church of England was in Great Britain. Officially, Judaism enjoyed equal standing to all the other religions, and more important, the huge number of Protestant denominations made the Jewish religion just one among many. The multiplication of Protestant sects prevented any one from dominating the others and encouraged a pluralistic tolerance of religious differences. That tolerance benefited American Jews. So had the public support offered by President George Washington in 1790 after his visit to the synagogue in Newport, Rhode Island. Washington declared that the new "good government" of the United States would guarantee "to bigotry no sanction, to persecution no assistance." The president added, however, that to thrive in the country, "the children of the stock of Abraham" must "demean themselves as good citizens."[8]

It's unlikely that Washington meant to impose any conditions on Jews that wouldn't apply to other citizens as well, but his statement left room for those who wanted to argue that Jews weren't good citizens—or that their religion, and later their "race," made them undeserving of the same citizens' rights that Protestants enjoyed. A significant, though varying, number of American Protestants would believe, well into the twentieth century and beyond, that "real Americans" were Protestants of Northern European stock. But this was rarely, if ever, the dominant view.

American religious diversity and tolerance encouraged the integration of Jews into the U.S. mainstream, and that integration, in turn, moved many Jews to mute the distinctiveness of dress, language, and religious expression that helped keep European Jews, especially those in the eastern half of the continent, separate from the rest of society. That distinctiveness was often used to justify discrimination and hostility against Jews. In the United States, Reform Judaism, which began in the early nineteenth century, imitated in certain ways the major Protestant denominations, holding religious services in English rather than Hebrew and introducing weekly sermons, music, and the integration of women as full members of a congregation.[9]

Perhaps most important, Jewish reformers anchored their religion firmly in the United States by deciding that America was the new Zion. By the mid-nineteenth century, this reform movement had largely abandoned one of the essential goals of traditional Judaism: the quest to return to the Holy Land and restore the great temple destroyed by Roman legions in 70 CE. Such a return was unnecessary because America, the land of religious freedom, had become the new homeland of the Jews. In that homeland, Jews no longer simmered in exile waiting for a messiah to lead them back to Jerusalem. The figure of the messiah, insisted reformist rabbis such as Isaac Mayer Wise and David Einhorn, had lost all anthropomorphic shape, its divinity having seeped into the Jewish people as a whole. The Jews were now a messianic people charged by God with bringing peace and justice to their new country and the world. And because the Jews no longer needed to restore the ancient temple of the Holy Land, their houses of worship in Charleston, Philadelphia, San Francisco, and New York could become temples in their

own right, which is what the reformers now called their synagogues.[10] In 1841, Gustavus Poznanski wrote of the Charleston
synagogue he led: "This synagogue is our *temple*, this city our
Jerusalem, this happy land [the United States] our *Palestine*."[11]
The idea of America as the new Palestine, combined with the
modernization (or Protestantization) of Jewish ritual and practice, likely kept a fair number of Jews from leaving their faith
behind and turned Judaism into a form of American religiosity
rather than a religion apart.

While American Jews moved closer to their Protestant counterparts, certain Protestant groups, especially evangelicals, moved
closer to American Jews. One key group, the Dispensationalists, became Zionists long before American Jews returned to
the idea at the end of the nineteenth century. Dispensationalism emerged in Britain in the 1830s as part of a broader funda-
mentalist, evangelical movement for reform within, or against,
the Anglican Church. This kind of fundamentalism crossed the
Atlantic after the Civil War and developed some popularity here
toward the end of the nineteenth century. The Dispensationalists' religious conservatism and commitment to the Bible's lit-
eral truth earned them a fair amount of support among those
who worried that mainstream Protestantism had made too
many accommodations to the irreligion and skepticism of the
modern world.[12]

Dispensationalists, like other fundamentalists, believed the
world was hurtling toward the apocalypse and that the world's
Jews would play the pivotal role in how the "end times" would
play out. Dispensationalists believed that God had created an

absolute distinction between Israel and the church, Jews and Christians. Jews were the earthly people, Christians the heavenly ones. But the premillennial world was all wrong, because Christians were living as an earthly people. As the end times approached, the true, believing Christians would be "raptured," that is, removed from the Earth, leaving the Jews in sole possession of the planet, just as God intended. With the Jews in charge, the state of Israel would be restored, and that restoration would open the way for the Antichrist to appear. This false god would promise to protect the Jews, and after lulling them to quiescence, treacherously turn on them by outlawing their religious practices and demanding that they worship him as God.

At this point, Christ would intervene, unleashing a series of horrible plagues and generating a cataclysmic battle, Armageddon, between the forces of darkness and God's people, the Jews. Christ's victory would restore the throne of David and usher in a thousand-year-long Jewish kingdom, as the Book of Revelation had prophesized. In this Jewish kingdom, the temple of Jerusalem would be restored, and Jesus, the new King of the Jews, would extend Jewish domination to the rest of the world. At the end of this Jewish millennium, Satan would make a last stand on Earth, and once defeated, he would retreat for good to Hell, leaving a Heaven on Earth for all those who had been saved. The Jews who had embraced Christ would join the raptured Christians in the eternal paradise that would mark the end of time.[13]

Except perhaps for the very end, when Jews would presumably have to stop being Jews, this is an extremely favorable view of the people of Abraham. It doesn't require, as some fundamentalists believed, that the Jews convert to Christianity to make the Second Coming possible, nor does it say that Jews will disappear from the Earth. Just the opposite: the Jews are destined for a thousand-year reign, and only after that will there be Heaven on Earth. The Jews are thus crucial for eternal salvation, which can't begin to occur until the state of Israel is restored. Such philosemitism was rare among Catholics, and it didn't characterize Protestants as a whole, but the Dispensationalists' eschatological views gave American Jews a measure of protection, even prestige.

Even so, the tolerance, even acceptance, Jews had enjoyed during the early American republic began to give way during and after the Civil War. The stereotypes became nastier and more prevalent, as Jews found themselves characterized as greedy, cunning, materialistic, and manipulative, as Shylocks dedicated to bilking Christians of their hard-earned money.[14] At the midcentury, Gentiles commonly called Jews "Christ-killers," and the word "Jew" had become an epithet used to condemn Christians deemed to have adopted evil Jewish ways. President John Tyler was denounced as an "accursed Jew," and enemies of General John C. Fremont, the Republican Party's first presidential candidate, rebaptized him as "a Jew." The word "Jew" now entered the English language as a verb or verb form: to "jew down" or "jewing" meant to haggle excessively or dishonestly. And no longer did "Jew" refer mainly to a member of a religious group. In some circles, the "Jew" was a swindler, a selfish rogue out for himself alone.[15]

It's unpleasant, of course, to be characterized in this way, but for the most part, Jews suffered little physical or material harm. They enjoyed freedom, citizenship, and civil liberties, not infrequently prospering and developing high standing in their communities. African Americans, both enslaved and free, suffered incomparably more, as did American Indians. As for Catholics, at midcentury, they found themselves hounded by members of the No-Nothing Party, named as such because adherents claimed to know nothing of the originally secret organization. In the mid-1850s, terrible anti-Catholic riots erupted in Manhattan, Brooklyn, Maine, Massachusetts, and St. Louis; altogether, dozens of Catholics were killed and scores seriously wounded. During the pre–Civil War decade, the No-Nothings elected 8 governors, 62 senators, and 104 members of the House. Once in office, No-Nothing officials forbade Catholic churches from purchasing property and kept policemen indoors as rioting engulfed cities and towns.[16] Once the Civil War began, the No-Nothings faded away, but the hostility to Catholics remained.

So did anti-Jewish prejudice. During the war, General Ulysses S. Grant infamously ordered the expulsion of all Jews from western Tennessee for supposedly having profiteered from the war—as if no non-Jews had done the same. President Lincoln quickly rescinded the order. In the North, Jews were sometimes denounced as insufficiently abolitionist, and in the South, as insufficiently favorable to slavery.[17]

After the war, and especially during the Gilded Age (1870s–1900), American clergymen, journalists, intellectuals, business-people, and many others became more preoccupied than ever before with what Europeans called the "Jewish question." Protestant leaders debated whether Jews were God's chosen people or the malignant remnant of a heretical people kept alive only to bear witness to the truth of Christ and the Jews' unsuccessful effort to betray him.[18] On the positive side, it wasn't just the somewhat idiosyncratic Dispensationalists who expressed philosemitic views; other, more mainstream, Protestant writers did as well. In the 1880s, Zebulon Vance, a senator and governor of North Carolina, praised the Jews as "descendants of those from whom we derive our civilization, kinsmen, after the flesh of Him whom we esteem as the Son of God and Saviour of men."[19] Vance's wasn't the dominant view, especially as the nineteenth century wore on, but he was far from alone in his defense of the Jews.[20]

Christian ambivalence toward American Jews coincided with ambivalence about the Jews' economic status and contributions, although anti-Jewish hostility mounted during the travails of the Gilded Age. On one hand, American commentators praised the Jews for their success in business—the United States, after all, was a country that valued entrepreneurship and the dynamism of industrial capitalism. But, on the other hand, Americans assessed bankers much less favorably, calling them unproductive and avaricious, people who benefited unjustly from the toil of others. It was well known that some of the world's top bankers were Jews—the Rothschilds, Bleichroders, Lazard brothers—and banking, in certain circles, came to be seen as a distinctively Jewish activity. This notion seemed plausible to many, given the Jews' traditional depiction as moneylenders and their reputation for cunning avariciousness. In English literature, Shylock had long been the paradigmatic Jew.

Such negative attitudes about "Jewish bankers" became increasingly common during the two decades of the Long Depression (1870s–1890s), when plummeting prices for agricultural products devastated U.S. farmers. To bolster those prices, Populists agitated to eliminate or reform the gold standard, which by limiting the amount of currency in circulation (paper money had to be backed by gold, an extremely rare commodity) proved highly deflationary. To raise prices, Populists, acting either on their own or through the Democratic Party, sought to create more money by coining silver and relaxing the gold standard.

Mainstream Republicans and Democrats steadfastly opposed the Populists' inflationary goals—business elites believed that inflation would reduce the value of their savings and investments—and they worried that the uncertainties of an untested bimetallic (gold/silver) monetary policy would harm international trade. When President Grover Cleveland called on the Rothschild Bank (plus J.P. Morgan & Co. and another Christian bank) to help save the gold standard in 1895, certain Populists pounced on the Rothschilds and blamed "Jewish finance" for the failure to alleviate the dire conditions of southern and western farmers.[21]

In 1896, William Jennings Bryan, the Democratic presidential candidate, appeared to endorse this populist imagery in his speech at the party convention: "You shall not press down upon the brow of labor this crown of thorns, you shall not crucify mankind upon a cross of gold." Since Christians commonly blamed Jews for the Crucifixion, and populists had connected Jews with the gold standard, American Jewish leaders found the speech offensive. Bryan had earlier said in Congress that the United Sates could not afford "to put ourselves in the hands of the Rothschilds." The Democratic tribune denied any anti-Jewish intent and would later sign a statement condemning Henry Ford's antisemitism.[22]

Americans in the 1890s—and since—have debated the extent to which Populism was antisemitic. An Associated Press reporter covering the Populist convention of 1896 found himself struck by "the extraordinary hatred of the Jewish race" among those in attendance.[23] But evidence abounds of far more benign Populist views of the Jews. In 1892, their presidential candidate, James B. Weaver, expressed admiration of the United States's diverse immigrant population, including the Jews, and referred to "the great bond of brotherhood which lies at the base of Christianity." In other populists, ambivalence reigned. The politician and writer Ignatius Donnelly thought Jews a once-noble race perverted by the persecution they had suffered at the hand of Christians. The Jews were not to blame. A Boston journalist displayed his ambivalence succinctly: "It is strange that a nation [i.e., the Jews] that boasts so many good traits should be so obnoxious."[24]

A key idea that emerged from the ambivalence of the "Populist moment" is that the "Hebrew race" threatened to take over the world—thanks to their financial and intellectual prowess.[25] The Jews, wrote Mark Twain in 1898, "were brighter and more talented than Christians and thus bested them in every endeavor where they competed," which is why Christians had long worked to exclude them from economic life. "The Jew is a money-getter," Twain added, and in "getting his money he is a very serious obstruction to less capable neighbors"—in part, Twain suggested, because the Jew shared none of the Christian's moral strictures. The Jew alone practiced "oppressive usury," while "arranging cunning contracts which leave him an exit but lock the other man in," and concocting "smart evasions which find him safe and comfortable just within the strict letter of the law, when court and jury know very well that he has violated the spirit of it."[26] For these and other reasons, wrote the prominent journalist Sydney Reid two years later, "The Jew is winning everywhere. By means fair or foul."[27]

This kind of rhetoric escalated in the new century. A prominent article in a 1907 issue of the popular *McClure's Magazine* asserted that "there is not the slightest doubt that in a few years the Jews will own the larger part of Manhattan Island" or that they will gain "absolute control of . . . nearly all medical and laboratory positions . . . a great majority of the engineering jobs [and] legal positions." Young Jewish men and women will likewise monopolize the city's clerical jobs.[28] Such writing revealed a worried admiration of Jews, a fear that if left to their own devices, they would turn the tables on Christian America.

Once again, it's crucial to add that this anti-Jewish rhetoric produced only a minuscule amount of violence against Jews. Hostile words can be demoralizing and psychologically damaging, but Irish Catholics, to say nothing of African Americans, terrorized by an epidemic of lynchings, endured verbal ugliness and also a fair amount of violence during the tense years of the American fin de siècle.[29] And of course, American Jews suffered immeasurably less than their European counterparts, who, during this same era of economic tribulation, faced pogroms and riots and one ritual murder accusation after another.

If American Jews experienced only minor violence in the late nineteenth and early twentieth centuries, they endured forms of social discrimination of unprecedented scale. That discrimination stemmed from two sources: the extraordinary success of Jews who had emigrated to the United States during the first sixty years of the nineteenth century, and the influx of about two million Eastern European Jews, 10 percent of all European immigrants, between 1880 and the early 1920s.[30] The language, dress, customs, and habits of the Jewish immigrants made them seem alien and undesirable, even to the mostly Cen-

tral European Jews who had come before them. The economically successful Jews evoked a new stereotype beyond the Jew as
Christ-killer, Christian-hater, and Shylock. This rags-to-riches
Jew was deemed a crude, ostentatious parvenu, an uncultivated
man avid to display his newfound riches.[31] Like most stereotypes, it contained a grain of truth. Those who had risen quickly
from humble beginnings could perhaps be forgiven for wanting
to advertise their success, and others could be forgiven for finding them annoying.

The upwardly mobile Jews rose quickly in a blossoming
new industrial society in which others were rising as well. Such
mobility commonly left members of older blue-blooded elites
behind and prevented wealthy Christians from distinguishing
themselves on economic grounds from newly wealthy Jews.
Such equalization, as Alexis de Tocqueville had pointed out, .
moved the old elites and other privileged people—in this case,
wealthy Christians—to distinguish themselves in other ways,
mainly by creating or re-creating exclusive privileges or prestigious institutions, organizations, and locales to which they
alone would be admitted.[32] During the Gilded Age, Christian
elites, whether declining or advancing, set themselves apart by
excluding Jews from clubs, resorts, hotels, schools, and other
places to which the Jews' wealth would have admitted them. In
some cases, institutions or establishments of mediocre renown
tried to boost their standing by excluding Jews and then touting
their exclusivity.[33]

Perhaps the most notorious early example of such anti-Jewish
discrimination came in 1877, when Judge Henry Hilton, owner
of the Grand Union Hotel in Saratoga Springs, New York, closed
his establishment to Joseph Seligman, a wealthy Jewish banker.

A friend of Abraham Lincoln and Ulysses S. Grant, Seligman had raised funds for the Union during the Civil War and helped refinance the war debt after 1865. The refusal to give Seligman a room caused a huge national scandal, with some editorialists saying that Hilton had a perfect right to keep Seligman—and other Jews—out. It seems that one of Hilton's motives was to restore the social exclusivity of Saratoga Springs, whose elite luster had faded somewhat in recent years.[34]

The effort backfired badly. Rather than keeping Jews away, Hilton's move only encouraged more of them to descend on his town. Jews bought several of the resort's leading hotels, and by the 1890s, half of Saratoga's summer residents were Jewish, the town itself divided between Jewish and non-Jewish establishments. With so many Jews in residence, Saratoga's aristocratic sheen dimmed for good. Even so, the Saratoga incident heralded a rash of discrimination against Jews in American vacation spots: the New Jersey shore, Coney Island, and the mountains of upstate New York. As in Saratoga Springs, the effort to exclude Jews resulted not in resorts free of Jews, but in the creation of Jewish and non-Jewish spaces within each locale.[35]

For the paragons of exclusivity, this outcome was doubtless better than nothing, and in other realms, they essentially succeeded in barring Jews altogether. By the late nineteenth century, elite social clubs had become prominent features of American cities, and having at first admitted prominent Jews, they began to reject them systematically in the 1880s. New York's Union League Club, for example, founded in 1863 by Union supporters in a largely Democratic city, refused in 1893 to admit Theodore Seligman even though his father had been one of the club's original members. Other leading social clubs throughout the East and Midwest followed suit, and by the 1890s, Jews found themselves with no alternative but to create clubs of their own.

Things became more complicated, and troubling, when Eastern European Jews developed a measure of economic success and wanted to join organizations and visit places outside their overcrowded downtown New York neighborhoods. Many of the relative newcomers from Eastern Europe seemed considerably more alien culturally than their German-Jewish predecessors, who had commonly joined reformed temples and conformed to dominant cultural norms. But by 1900, Eastern European Jews vastly outnumbered their German counterparts, and in the minds of a great many Gentiles, it was the former who represented the whole of American Jewry.

Discrimination now reached into most realms of American society. Exclusive boarding schools erected narrow quotas that kept Jewish students to a minimum, while country clubs, Masonic lodges, and a variety of long-integrated resorts now kept Jews away. When Jews bought into a resort, as they had in Saratoga Springs, Christians fled to other places, turning once-swank resorts like Lakewood, New Jersey, into undesirable (at least to Gentiles) Jewish towns.[36] The irony in these developments, as John Higham makes clear, was that the very American freedom that allowed prosperous individuals to move unhindered around the country—there was nothing like Russia's Pale of Settlement where most Russian Jews were confined—also fostered the social discrimination that compromised this freedom.[37]

Other forms of anti-Jewish discrimination included efforts to prevent Jews from buying or renting property in certain neighborhoods, limiting their enrollment in colleges and universities, and, within those institutions, barring Jews from prestigious fraternities. Eventually, Jewish students created fraternities of their own, replicating the socioreligious segregation that already existed in clubs and resorts—and was underway in cities and towns, where separate Jewish and non-Jewish neighborhoods increasingly became the norm. The greatest exceptions to this norm existed in California and in the South. In San Francisco, social discrimination targeted Asians above all, and in the general hostility to Chinese and Japanese immigrants, Jews, relatively few in number, mostly escaped biased treatment. The same was true of the South, where Jim Crow made African Americans the outcast group and counted the Jews as white.[38]

The situation was altogether different in the East and Midwest, where few Asians lived and blacks remained a small minority before their great migration northward in the 1910s. Until then, the outcast groups comprised European immigrants from Ireland, Italy, Russia, Greece, and Eastern Europe. If Jews faced more discrimination than other people, it was a difference in severity, not in kind. Jews, that is, were not, as yet, singled out as a "race" more loathsome or dangerous than Italians or Greeks, but rather as a people that had grown too wealthy, too fast, and thus required a special effort to keep them in their place. So, if other European immigrant groups faced less severe discrimination than the Jews, it was because the Jews' economic success gave them the means to take vacations, pay club dues, send their children to college, and move away from overcrowded urban neighborhoods. The only way for Gentiles to maintain their predominance was to create artificial barriers against Jews who wanted to enjoy the privileges of the new American prosperity, a prosperity to which they had contributed far beyond their numbers.

Many Jews doubtless found this social discrimination humiliating, unjust, and unworthy of the "land of the free." But Jews could, at least, compensate for it by establishing institutions of their own. What proved harder to circumvent and appeared more threatening was the newer, racially tinged antisemitism that emerged during and after the First World War. By then, the two million Jews who had recently flooded into the United States appeared to a fair number of native-born Protestants as unassimilable, dangerous politically, and, above all, a threat to their perceived American way of life. Such nativist views played a key role in the revival of the Ku Klux Klan, which grew from a tiny fringe group in 1915 to one of the largest organizations in the United States a decade later. The Klan proved to be more anti-Catholic than antisemitic, but together with Henry Ford's powerful anti-Jewish campaign of the 1920s, the KKK made life more uncomfortable for American Jews than ever before in the nation's history.

The revived Ku Klux Klan emerged in a postwar America suffering the aftershocks of the country's first major military engagement overseas. The war had produced an intense nationalist reaction among all parties to the conflict, including the United States. Already in 1915, two years before the American entry into the war, former president Theodore Roosevelt coined the term "One Hundred Percent Americanism" to distinguish the "real Americans" who had deep roots in this country from the newcomers who didn't fully belong. Meanwhile, other political leaders, journalists, and prominent figures began to say that immigrants or "hyphenated Americans" might be more loyal to their countries of origin than to the United States. Immigrants, that is, were a potential fifth column during the war, and only native-born Protestant Americans could be trusted as genuine patriots. After the war, President Woodrow Wilson adopted this point of view, declaring during his futile campaign to ratify the Treaty of Versailles, "the most un-American thing in the world is a hyphen" and "any man who carries a hyphen around with him carries a dagger that he is ready to plunge into the vitals of the republic."[39]

The Russian Revolution of 1917 had intensified the suspicion of immigrants, especially those from Russia and Eastern Europe, now seen as Bolsheviks in disguise. Policemen invaded their meetings, rounding up some 3,000 people in the "Palmer Raids" of early January 1920. Many were thrown in jail and more than a few deported. Since Jews were heavily represented among the immigrants suspected of disloyalty or subversive beliefs, "one hundred percent Americanists" often singled them out and increasingly found them an alien, inferior group.[40] The hostility to immigrants culminated in the Johnson-Reed, or Immigration, Act of 1924, which banned the immigration of Arabs and Asians and tightly limited the number of Eastern and Southern Europeans who could move to the United States.

Jews were far from the only group deemed insufficiently American. A great many Protestants considered their Catholic countrymen more loyal to the pope than to the president of the United States, and the 1920s saw a powerful hostility between the two groups. That hostility came to a head in the sharp conflict over the Eighteenth Amendment (1919), which outlawed the "manufacture, sale, or transportation of intoxicating liquors." Protestants generally supported Prohibition and Catholics generally did not.

Meanwhile, African Americans, having contributed mightily to the war effort in 1917 and 1918, demanded a measure of equality in return. For those demands, they faced a terrible wave of violence instigated by whites. Rioting stretched across urban America during the "red summer" of 1919, known as such for the fires that blazed through black communities. Some of the worst rioting took place in Chicago, and then two years later in Tulsa, Oklahoma, which became the scene of the most intense white-on-black violence in American history. The Tulsa pogroms left as many as 150 people dead and the large black community of Greenwood reduced to smoking ruins.[41]

The postwar conflicts stemmed not only from the nationalist passions unleashed during the Great War but also from the deep changes that had altered the very essence of the United States. No longer was it a largely rural, agricultural country whose population hailed mainly from Northern Europe and the British Isles. The United States had become a powerful, populous, industrial nation whose inhabitants resided primarily in cities and had become extraordinarily diverse. Catholics now stood out as the largest single religious denomination— Protestants, still the majority of the country, were divided into a multitude of sects. Jews, though only 3 percent of the populace, seemed a much bigger group, concentrated as they were in America's largest cities. At the same time, African Americans had migrated en masse to the North, no longer willing to endure the constraints of Jim Crow, and women had demanded and obtained the right to vote.

These deep changes sparked a potent reaction on the part of traditionalists, who longed for an idealized old United States, and a variety of other individuals and groups that feared they were being left behind. The reactions took their most extreme, divisive form in a new version of the long-defunct Ku Klux Klan.

The original Klan had emerged from the swirling anger, resentment, and disappointment that followed the South's defeat in the Civil War. For a significant number of southern whites, the world had been turned upside down, as Reconstruction governments imposed by the victorious North allowed newly enfranchised African Americans to hold public office and exercise power locally in ways unimaginable before 1865. The KKK was established to terrorize blacks and restore the old status quo by force.

Klan members donned face-covering hoods and long white robes partly to disguise themselves and partly to inspire fear. They murdered elected black officials and their white supporters and killed African Americans as they attempted to vote. By the time the U.S. government suppressed the Klan in 1871, the damage had been done. Fearing violence against them, blacks increasingly stayed away from the polls, and when Reconstruction ended in 1877, white supremacy returned in force to the South.

Although the KKK had been outlawed, it lived on in memory. It took literary form in Thomas Dixon's 1905 novel, *The Clansman*, which itself became the basis for D. W. Griffith's landmark 1915 film, *The Birth of a Nation*. The movie's technical virtuosity brilliantly served its racist message. In a series of visually stunning scenes without precedent in earlier films, Griffith portrayed the Klan's hooded members as fearless heroes who rescued white southern women from the immoral savagery of black men.[42]

The film proved wildly popular, as millions of Americans traveled long distances and endured endless lines to see it. President Wilson arranged for it to be shown in the White House, and members of Congress and the Supreme Court attended a special elite screening. Critics hailed the film as a masterpiece that promised to transform the cinema from lowbrow entertainment to an art form appealing to the middle class. Still, there were writers at the time who abhorred the film's racist message, and the National Association for the Advancement of Colored People (NAACP), founded in 1909, organized protests against it.[43]

But the film's popularity and the official sanction that the president seemed to give it prevented most opponents of the film from being heard. A Methodist Episcopal minister named William J. Simmons found himself so moved by *The Birth of a Nation* that he decided to revive the Ku Klux Klan, copying the hooded costumes from the film. He organized a cross burning, also copied from the movie, atop Stone Mountain (Georgia) on Thanksgiving eve 1915 and limited membership to native-born white Protestants, excluding not only African Americans but Catholics and Jews as well. Simmons saw the Klan as a hyper-patriotic organization dedicated to traditional values and to preserving the country's Protestant, Northern European roots.

The KKK started slowly with just a few thousand members, but it began to attract widespread support in 1920, as the conflicts of the postwar years engulfed the nation. To advertise the organization, Simmons turned to a pair of publicists, Edward Clarke and Elizabeth Tyler, who understood the techniques of mass propaganda and the power of the press. Clarke and Tyler claimed allegiance to the goals of the Klan but also saw it as a way to make money. Each new member was assessed a ten-dollar initiation fee ($130 today), four dollars of which went to the local leader (kleagle) who recruited him. Another $1.50 flowed to the Klan's regional and state officials, while Simmons, Clarke, and Tyler received the rest. At every level, KKK officials had a strong financial incentive to bring in new members, and as the number of adherents swelled, so did the treasury of the KKK. At the height of the organization's popularity in 1924, with its national membership reaching perhaps four million, the Klan brought in more than twenty-five million dollars (a staggering $353 million today).[44] Simmons and his colleagues also made money by monopolizing the production of Klan robes and hoods and marking up the price by more than a factor of three.[45]

Already by 1921, the Hooded Empire, as it was called, possessed the means to publish its own newspapers and magazines, which spread its ideology and brought in new members. No longer was the Klan primarily a terrorist organization, and it targeted errant whites more than blacks. Violence against African Americans was so widespread in the 1920s that the Klan didn't need to join in, although sometimes its members participated, unmasked, in lynch mobs and urban riots.[46] Still, in the deep South, KKK members were merciless toward African Americans who transgressed the sexual barrier between whites and blacks. In one notorious case, Klansmen from Houston castrated an African American dentist who had been fined for having sexual relations with a white woman. But even in the South and Southwest, where black men rarely took the risk of involvement with white women, the hooded order mostly targeted white men, and occasionally women, for sexual impropriety. In Houston, one white sexual offender was castrated, but most of the Klan's violent punishments for supposed moral transgressions took the form of whipping, branding, and tarring and feathering.[47]

Such awful escapades earned the Klan unfavorable scrutiny from the big-city press. In 1921, the *New York World* ran a series of articles exposing the misdeeds of the KKK. Reprinted in papers around the country, the series triggered a lengthy congressional investigation. The inquiry backfired, however, against the opponents of the hooded order. Simmons came off in his testimony as sincere, upstanding, and respectable—as a real American with America's best interests at heart. The Klan leader managed to avert a crisis but was unable to make his leadership position secure. In November 1922, a Dallas dentist named Hiram Wesley Evans staged a coup against Simmons and his sidekicks Clarke and Tyler, ousting them from the organization and installing himself as imperial wizard.

Once in power, Evans moved quickly to disassociate the KKK from violence and make the organization into a mass, mainstream organization. By 1923, the KKK had become an extremist variant of the fraternal associations—Masons, Elks, Lions—popular at the time, and a fair number of Masons also joined the Klan. In Texas, Oregon, and Indiana, the Klan became so mainstream that congressmen, senators, and even a governor or two either belonged to the group or looked favorably on it.[48] The KKK endorsed local and statewide efforts to back public schools and prohibit Catholic ones, and, in general, it sought to uphold Prohibition and to enforce "traditional" morals, which it believed were under threat from Hollywood, jazz music and dancing, the "Jewish press," and urban culture. The Klan campaigned against the immigration of "mongrel races" and went on the offensive against Catholics and, to a lesser extent, Jews.

Calling the United States a "Protestant-Christian nation," leaders of the hooded order strongly supported the Immigration Act of 1924 on the grounds that most of those entering the country were Catholics and Jews, people whose religion and supposed racial inferiority had already debased America's pure, Nordic stock. In keeping with ideas about race influential in the early twentieth century, the Klan defined American identity in terms of what we would nowadays call race, religion, and ethnicity. For the KKK, only native-born Protestants of Northern European heritage could be true Americans. Eastern and Southern Europeans, whether Catholics or Jews, could not. It went without saying that people of African or Asian heritage could never be American.

Since Chinese immigration had been banned in 1882 and African Americans subdued by pogroms and institutionalized discrimination, the Klan zeroed in on Catholics, whose growing numbers seemed the greatest threat. Propagandists for the hooded order began with long-standing anti-Catholic themes, especially the notion that priests and nuns engaged in immoral acts behind their cloistered walls and that Catholics wanted to subordinate the United States to the Vatican. Catholic countries, they said, were inferior to Protestant ones, and American Cath-

The Klan goes mainstream in the 1920s.

olics wanted to hand the country over to foreigners and debase its culture all the more.[49]

In the early 1920s, the Klan's national headquarters circulated a series of talking points against Catholics and Catholicism, declaring that "the pope is a political autocrat" who enthroned "one hundred and sixteen princes of his government [i.e., cardinals] . . . in our cities." These princes ensured that "courts here enforce[ed] the canon law" while controlling "the daily and magazine press." Beyond these common points disseminated nationally, regional Klansmen were obsessed with the notion that the pope planned to build an American Vatican in Washington, D.C. And the rumor circulated widely in the Invisible Empire that the basements of Catholic churches had been stocked with weapons in preparation for a war to the death against Protestant America. Each time a son was born to a Catholic family, a new weapon was supposedly added to the stock.[50] This rumor didn't dip to the depravity of Jewish ritual murder, often said to take place in synagogue basements, but it showed a breathtaking fear of and antagonism toward Catholics.

One key unintended consequence of the hooded order's anti-Catholicism was to bring together Catholics of different national origins, especially Irish and Italian and, given the Klan's Protestant exclusivity, to commit many American Catholics to pluralism. Under collective assault in the 1920s, Catholics, Jews, African Americans, and labor organizations made common cause against the KKK. So did Protestant opponents of the Klan; if all Klan members were Protestants, not all Protestants sympathized with the group.[51]

American Jews benefited from the pluralist tolerance of the Catholic and Protestant enemies of the Klan, for Jews also found themselves in the crosshairs of the Hooded Empire. As the KKK grew in the early 1920s, it drew on the ambient antisemitism of those years. That antisemitism had been intensified by postwar suspicion of foreigners, by the Russian Revolution, whose opponents often identified Bolsheviks with Jews, and by prominent antisemites such as the populist demagogue Tom Watson and the famous automaker Henry Ford.

Watson had stoked hatred of Jews during and after the trial of Leo Frank, a Jewish factory manager in Atlanta accused in

1913 of murdering a fourteen-year-old worker named Mary Phagan.[52] The evidence against Frank was thin at best, but the prosecution successfully coached Jim Conley, a black employee of the factory, to testify against him. The all-white jury credited Conley's testimony over that of the accused northern Jew, and Frank was convicted largely on the strength of Conley's words. After the trial, Frank's supporters, including the influential Hearst newspapers, undertook a campaign to have the verdict revised. Watson led the effort to sustain Frank's conviction and in the process mobilized a wide variety of antisemitic stereotypes, especially the supposed power of moneyed Jews and the newspapers and politicians they had bought. It's notable that Watson never accused Frank of ritual murder, even though all the ingredients were there: a young Christian girl killed by a Jew and her quasi-deification by fervent throngs after the event. Watson may never have heard of the ritual murder accusation, given its absence from American history, or if he had, he might have thought it wouldn't ring any bells among Phagan's supporters.

Inevitably, Georgia's governor, John M. Slaton, found himself drawn into the controversy surrounding Frank's conviction. After carefully studying the case, he commuted Frank's sentence. On hearing that news, a mob of "Mary's people" broke into the jail where Frank was being held, kidnapped the terrified businessman, and hanged him from a tree. Even though the revived Klan took shape in Atlanta in 1915, there is no evidence that the fledgling organization was behind the lynching. Watson clearly urged it on, but Phagan's supporters would likely have turned to rough justice without him. After Frank's limp body was cut from its noose, a joyous crowd kicked and stomped it and almost succeeded in cutting it to pieces. No member of the mob was ever tried for Frank's murder—perhaps because no jury would have convicted anyone for the crime. Afterwards, Watson wrote, "In putting the Sodomite murderer to death the Vigilance Committee [lynch mob] has done what the Sheriff should have done, if [Governor] Slaton had not been in the mold of Benedict Arnold. LET JEW LIBERTINES TAKE NOTICE! Georgia is not for sale to rich criminals."[53]

Although the ritual murder accusation didn't come up in the Leo Frank case, it joined a long line of politically significant false accusations that had punctuated U.S. history. The most notorious of these cases is doubtless the accusation of witchcraft leveled against some 200 people in and around Salem, Massachusetts, in 1692 and 1693.[54] Fourteen women and five men were executed for the supposed crime, and others died in jail. Several of those accused confessed to being witches and implicated other people, some of them longtime antagonists of their families. These confessions, as Judge Joseph Cotton wrote in the 1740s, were "not worth a Straw; for many times they are obtain'd by foul means, by force or torment, by Surprise, by flattery, by Distraction . . . or in hopes of a longer time to live, or to dy an easier death. For any body would chuse rather to be hanged than to be burnt."[55] The "witches'" confessions recalled those given by European Jews subjected to judicial torture in ritual murder cases.

Awful as the Salem executions were, a series of false accusations a half-century later took a far greater toll. In 1741, magistrates in New York City condemned some 200 enslaved black men and women for supposedly plotting to incinerate the young metropolis and murder its white inhabitants. Punishments were harsh: thirteen black men burned at the stake; another seventeen hanged; two white men and two white women, judged the ringleaders, hanged; eighty-four black men and women sold to Caribbean owners whose plantation slaves survived about ten years on average. As in Salem, most of the New York slaves found guilty of arson and attempted murder had confessed, but the confessions had been coerced or given in the belief that leniency would result. There was no slave conspiracy to torch New York.[56]

The fear of slave revolts persisted into the nineteenth century, and slaves continued to be falsely accused of incitement or worse. After the Civil War, the false accusations against African Americans shifted from rebellion to rape and murder. Beginning in the 1870s, the all-too-frequent lynchings of black men found their justification in the purported need to protect white women from black lust. Although black-on-white rapes doubtlessly occurred, they were uncommon. Most sexual assault charges against black men were false.[57]

So were most accusations of blacks for the murder of whites, which didn't prevent a false murder charge from being an even more common pretext for lynching than the accusation of rape.[58] If most victims of lynch mobs were black, Leo Frank did not escape this fate. His antagonist Tom Watson, having rejoiced in the crowd's vigilante justice, graduated from the populism of the pre–First World War period to the nativism of the 1920s. Early in that decade, he expressed sympathy for the revived Ku Klux Klan, whose national leaders showed unabashed hostility to the Jews, now considered a racial rather than a religious group.

The imperial wizard, Hiram Evans, deemed the Jews an "absolutely unblendable element," adding, "in a thousand years of continuous residence," they would never "form basic attachments [to] American society and institutions."[59] Evans would later concede that German Jews might eventually be assimilable, although Eastern European Jews, whom he dismissed as "Judaized Mongols," could never become Americans.[60] They were thus inherently unpatriotic, which is why the hooded order worked hard to ban Jewish immigration, which mostly came from Eastern Europe. These Jews were "internationalists," not nationalists, and for that reason, KKK spokesmen endorsed Henry Ford's antisemitic campaign against the "International Jew," whose "money grasping" had led to the First World War. And like Ford, Klansmen denounced the international Jew as, at once, capitalist and Bolshevik, as posing a dire threat to Christian civilization.

Klan members were especially hostile to "Jew Hollywood," whose immoral motion pictures corrupted "one hundred percent American" women and children. One unsubtle Klan pamphlet bore the title "Jew Movies urging sex vice: Rome [i.e., Catholics] and Judah at work to Pollute Young America." It denounced "the poisonous flood of filthy Jewish suggestion [that] has been paralyzing the moral sense of America's children."[61] The hooded order found Charlie Chaplin's 1923 film *The Pilgrim* particularly offensive. In this unheralded silent feature, Chaplin stars as an escaped convict who steals a minister's clothing after shedding his prison garb. The other characters see him as a real Protestant clergyman, and the plot revolves around his mistaken identity. This narrative device infuriated Klan spokesmen, who launched a powerful campaign against the film. The *Imperial Night Hawk* denounced Chaplin as a "vulgar" Jewish comedian whose "burlesque" antics outrageously mocked a Protestant man of the cloth. Chaplin was born to Christian parents and considered himself an agnostic, but he never responded to antisemitic slurs by referring to his non-Jewish origins. Several states banned *The Pilgrim* on the strength of the Klan's critique.[62]

As if Hollywood's moral corruption wasn't bad enough, the KKK also accused Jews of kidnapping Protestant women for their "white-slave dens." Klansmen routinely claimed that Jewish men lusted for Protestant women, hoping to intermarry with them and to "miscegenate" by producing "mixed-race" children. On the subject of children, members of the hooded order claimed that Jews compromised the American educational system by inventing evolutionary theory and teaching it in public schools. After the Scopes "Monkey Trial," KKK leaders praised William Jennings Bryan, who had argued the case against evolution, as "the greatest Klansman of our time."[63]

Ugly as these comments were, they were mild in comparison to the statements of European antisemites like Drumont and Rohling, who harped on Jewish ritual murder and encouraged violence against Jewish communities. The Klan worried more about Catholics than Jews; Catholics represented a far larger proportion of the American population.[64] This focus on Catholics was perhaps small consolation for American Jews, who deeply resented the KKK's propaganda denying their belonging to the American community, but Jewish leaders understood that the hooded order didn't pose a mortal threat.[65]

Such was especially true of the second half of the 1920s, when the Klan's membership and influence precipitously declined. Already in the early 1920s, the hooded order had faced opposition from Catholic, African American, Jewish, and labor organizations. That opposition began to take a toll when several prominent KKK leaders were exposed as hypocrites, either for public intoxication or for various sexual transgressions. The organization also suffered from its rapid success. It grew so quickly between 1921 and 1924 that its national leaders lacked the institutional means to control its state and local branches and leaders, many of whom had their own sources of power and support. For the same reason, the hooded order could develop no coherent connective tissue of ideas that might have helped hold the organization together. And when prosperity returned to the United States in the mid-1920s, Americans gradually forgot the resentments of the immediate postwar years, and many of those who had joined the hooded order felt that they no longer needed it. The Klan would enjoy a brief resurgence during the election of 1928, which pitted the Protestant Herbert Hoover against the Catholic Al Smith, but after the contest was decided, the Klan faded away.[66]

From the Jews' point of view, Henry Ford represented a far greater threat than the KKK. By the early 1920s, Ford had become a great American folk hero revered for building the mass-produced cars that middle-class people could afford, but also for appearing to embody traditional, small-town values. He seemed both a great innovator and a reassuring traditionalist, a man who got Americans to spend their money while extolling the simple, unadorned life. In his many public statements, Ford appealed to the common man, common sense, and the commonplace. He distrusted elites, urbanites, and intellectuals and claimed to value folk wisdom over book learning, his own hunches over what passed for scientific truth. He had come from small-town Protestant America, and he disliked many of

Henry Ford

the changes mass immigration had wrought. He also disliked and distrusted many of the immigrants themselves, especially the Jews among them.[67]

Shortly after Ford's unsuccessful bid for the United States Senate in 1918, he bought a failing small-town newspaper, the *Dearborn Independent*, in an effort to keep one foot in the political arena. The big-city press, he said, was "owned body and soul by bankers"—the same people who had supposedly engineered his political defeat—and the *Independent* would give the country an independent voice—namely, his. Every day, the paper ran an editorial that reflected Ford's views, although the pieces were written by the journalist William J. Cameron. Readers were attracted to Ford's ideas and also to the paper's articles about politics, the economy, technology, foreign countries, music, and film. The *Independent* proved hugely successful, its circulation hitting 900,000 a day in 1926.[68] For comparison, the circulation that year of the daily *New York Times* was about 356,000 and the Sunday *Times* 610,000.[69]

After a year of editorializing about this and that, Ford decided, seemingly out of the blue, to undertake a campaign against the Jews. The decision moved his editor to resign and eventually mired the automaker in the greatest controversy of his life. Ford entitled his campaign "The International Jew: The World's Problem" and published a front-page article every week criticizing and denigrating the Jews. The articles were written by Cameron, but Ford made it clear that they reflected his personal views.

Henry Ford's press campaign against the Jews

It's unclear what motivated this antisemitic campaign, and many observers have been mystified by it. Ford's recent biographer, Steven Watts, attributes it to three sources: a populist disdain for bankers and moneymen; his opposition to the U.S. participation in the Great War, a conflict caused, he said, by German-Jewish bankers; and a cultural conservatism consonant with the heightened nationalism and nativism of the postwar years. In this fraught climate, a variety of conservative commentators idealized the United States's preindustrial, small-town, Anglo-Protestant past. Ford also seems to have been influenced by Ernest G. Liebold, his business secretary and office manager, who had read *The Protocols of the Elders of Zion*. This notorious antisemitic forgery recounted a meeting in which Jewish leaders devised a plan to dominate the world.[70] It was pure fiction, but Liebold apparently took the *Protocols* at face value, and so did Henry Ford.

The automaker's front-page articles harped on the supposed Jewish effort to dominate the world and traded in the stock stereotypes long used to denigrate Jews. Members of this "race," Ford said, had a "distaste for hard or violent physical labor," a "capacity for exploitation," a "shrewdness and astuteness in speculation and money matters generally," and "an Oriental love of display." Ford included some positive stereotypes as well: "a strong family sense," "a marked religious instinct," "a very high average of intellectual ability." But he was most exercised about the Jews' putative financial prowess, urging the American public to examine the "money aristocracy" they had created before it was too late. From these stereotypes, Ford concluded that "the International Jew and his satellites [were] the conscious enemies of all that Anglo-Saxons mean by civilization."[71]

The titles of Ford's weekly articles highlighted his anti-Jewish paranoia: "Does Jewish Power Control the World Press?"; "Jewish Testimony in Favor of Bolshevism"; "Jewish Rights Clash with American Rights"; "How Jewish International Finance Functions." Ford even decried the "Jewish Degradation of American Baseball," not to mention the Jews' responsibility for the evils of jazz—apparently with people like Irving Berlin, Al Jolson, and George Gershwin in mind.[72]

In one of his most disturbing articles, Ford allied himself ideologically with Germany's fledgling national socialist movement, to which Ford sent Liebold as an emissary in the early 1920s.[73] Like the young Hitler, Ford claimed that "the collapse which has come since the armistice [in Germany], and the revolution from which they are being prevented a recovery, are the result of Jewish intrigue." The Jews, Ford said, had been able to destroy the once-great German state, because "Judaism is the most closely organized power on earth, even more than the British Empire." Resembling that empire, but supplanting it, a Jewish "world government," its capitals now in London, New York, and Paris, didn't need a standing army or navy: "Its fleet is the British fleet, which guards from hindrance the progress of the all-Jewish world economy."[74]

Turning to the United States, Ford's ghostwriter pointed to a long history of Jewish domination, a history that began, he said, with the Dutch settlement of New York. "Here in the United States," Ford/Cameron declared, "it is the fact of this remarkable minority—a sparse Jewish ingredient of three per cent in a nation of 110,000,000—attaining in 50 years a degree of control that would be impossible to a ten times larger group of any other race."[75] This outsized Jewish control constituted for Ford the essence of "the Jewish question": how did Americans allow such a small group to gain so much power, and what could be done to stem it?

Much of this discussion slides into an envious admiration for the Jews, who in business are "naturally quicker than most other men," and in general are more intelligent, more resourceful, and more disciplined than everyone else.[76] Such, of course, is true of much antisemitic writing, which commonly attributes extraordinary powers to Jews, whose "innate gifts," as Ford's mouthpiece put it, have enabled them to amass enormous wealth and power. It isn't antisemitic to say such things, Ford maintained, because they reflect the truth of Jewish domination.

Ford concluded his long series of articles with a warning to Jews to develop "a sense of social responsibility," to rein themselves in before others did it for them. As for his "Address to Gentiles on the Jewish Problem," Ford urged his fellows to be vigilant—but not violent—in curbing the Jews' excessive power. Real Americans must remove Jewish themes from books and movies and see to it that the church is "unJudaized and Christianized" and "the Government . . . Americanized."[77]

This anti-Jewish tirade surprised many people and generated both outrage and delight. Over one hundred religious, intellectual, and political leaders signed a statement condemning Ford's articles, and there was pressure to remove the *Independent* from public libraries and car dealerships. Louis Marshall and other prominent Jews denounced the pieces as unbecoming and un-American.[78] But plenty of people apparently approved of what Ford had to say: the circulation of his paper spiked upward during his antisemitic campaign.[79]

Given Ford's stature in postwar America, Marshall worried that the automaker's campaign could trigger a European-style antisemitism until then absent from American life; the usually cautious Marshall decided to confront Ford head-on. The Jewish leader began by organizing an effort to demonstrate the speciousness of *The Protocols of the Elders of Zion*, the pamphlet that had so deeply influenced Ford and Liebold. Marshall then enlisted the non-Jewish journalist John Spargo to compose a critique of the *Independent*'s antisemitic articles and later wrote a critique of his own.[80] These efforts paid off: newspapers from coast to coast ran editorials denouncing Ford's antisemitism and calling on him to halt his scurrilous campaign. But in the automaker's view, the editorials against him proved the point he was trying to make; namely, that Jews like Marshall controlled the press and dominated the United States.

Ford remained unbowed and even upped the ante. In 1924, the *Independent* published a series of twenty-one articles accusing Aaron Sapiro, a successful attorney and agricultural entrepreneur, of plotting to turn the U.S. economy over to international Jewish financiers. Sapiro had organized sixty-six farm cooperatives, whose annual receipts topped $400 million, and Ford launched an antisemitic barrage against him. This campaign resembled earlier ones against Herman Bernstein, editor of the *Jewish Tribune*, and against army captain Robert Rosenbluth, whom Ford had falsely accused of murdering his commanding officer during the war.[81]

In February 1925, Sapiro sued Ford for libel, claiming damages to his reputation and his livelihood worth one million dollars, a spectacular sum for the time. Ford's attorneys succeeded in delaying the trial for two years, and when it finally opened in March 1927, the automaker's team of eight lawyers argued that the *Independent* had truthfully portrayed Sapiro as "a grafter, faker, fraud, and cheat." And, in any case, the newspaper had leveled Ford's attacks against Jews as a race and not against any Jewish individual. This defense mirrored the argument made by Plamondon's attorney in Quebec more than a decade earlier: no law prohibited the criticism of a group. Ford's attorneys added the false claim that although the *Independent* belonged to Ford, he played no role in shaping its editorial policy.

Sapiro's attorney decided to break down these arguments by calling Ford himself to the stand. But the automaker did everything in his power to avoid testifying. He had come off badly in an earlier libel suit and feared the same thing would happen again. He hid from subpoena servers for weeks and then claimed a serious disability after his sideswiped car careened off the road and into a nest of trees. Ford's attorneys said he was too injured to appear in court, but it later became clear that Ford had staged the crash both to avoid testifying and to step up his attacks on American Jews. Newspapers sympathetic to Ford claimed that Jewish assassins had run him off the road in a failed effort to kill him: "Plot to Assassinate Ford Seen" read one headline, and "Ford Injured by Assassins" screamed another.[82]

When Sapiro's attorney demanded Ford's medical records, the automaker admitted that there had been no assassination attempt and that he would recover enough to testify soon. But Ford had had enough. He directed his attorneys to negotiate a settlement with Sapiro and, more startlingly, agreed to shut down the *Dearborn Independent* and apologize for his antisemitic slurs. The automaker apparently decided that the Sapiro case, like his other anti-Jewish attacks, had needlessly damaged his reputation at a time when a major business move had already generated a raft of negative publicity. His decision to replace the Model T with the Model A required the Ford Motor Company to close its assembly lines for six months and temporarily lay off thousands of workers.[83]

Ford's representatives approached leaders of the two major Jewish organizations, the American Jewish Committee and the American Jewish Congress, hoping to work out a deal. As president of the American Jewish Committee, Marshall took over the negotiations and insisted that Ford compensate Sapiro handsomely and, more important, that he issue a formal apology to the Jewish community. Ford agreed to both. In his apology, written by Marshall and signed verbatim by Ford, the automaker said it was his "duty as an honorable man to make amends for the wrong done to the Jews as fellow men and brothers," and he retracted "so far as lies within my power the offensive charges laid at their door."[84]

For American Jews, Ford's apology ended what was the most sustained, and damaging, anti-Jewish attack in the nation's history. Marshall had played a crucial role in this successful outcome, but he had not single-handedly halted Ford's campaign. The persistent opposition of prominent Americans, and especially of Hearst-owned newspapers, had kept the automaker on the defensive throughout the 1920s, his obnoxious ideas contained. Even with the postwar resurgence of nativism and the Ku Klux Klan, most Americans had no taste for the antisemitic political movements, with their demagogic politicians, mass protests, and street violence, that were roiling Europe and Quebec.

Still, Marshall gave himself a fair amount of credit, and his ability to have Ford sign the abject apology he had composed may have gone to his head. A year later, he would insist on a similar apology from Massena's leaders, an apology that would be far more difficult to extract.

Chapter 5

THE ELECTION OF 1928

That the Massena blood libel took place in 1928 was no accident. It occurred at the beginning of one of the ugliest and most intense electoral campaigns in United States history. That campaign pitted the old-stock Protestant Herbert Hoover, who represented the Republican Party, against the Irish Catholic Al Smith, who represented the Democrats. Although Hoover himself didn't attack Smith's Catholicism, his surrogates and other Republicans claimed that the Democratic candidate's religion made him a danger to the country. The campaign was scurrilous but mercifully short—back then, presidential races didn't begin in earnest until Labor Day. It was anything but sweet.

One irony of this prejudice-laced, hostile campaign is that both candidates were decent men with impressive personal and political résumés. Both had worked their way up from rela-

Herbert Hoover, 1928

tively humble beginnings, remained untainted by corruption, and used their skills and positions to do things for ordinary people. But each appeared to stand for an opposing version of the United States. The Republican candidate seemed to embody the culture and values of rural, Protestant America, while the Democratic candidate epitomized an urban America crowded with immigrants and a large number of Catholics and Jews.

The two men were born just a year apart, Smith in New York City in 1873, Hoover in West Branch, Iowa, in 1874. Orphaned at age nine, Hoover ping-ponged from one relative to another before getting some direction in life from an uncle who owned a real estate firm in Portland, Oregon. Hoover took to the business and also became interested in mining and engineering. He had the intelligence and family resources to attend Stanford University, joining its first undergraduate class in 1891.

Hoover's professional career began in Australia and took him to several parts of the globe. He proved successful not just as a mining engineer but also as a financier and troubleshooter for new and failing firms, and he had visited Massena's Alcoa factory in 1905.[1] Hoover amassed a large fortune but became bored with business and retired at age forty. Fortuitously, his

Al Smith, 1928

retirement coincided with the outbreak of the Great War, which gave him the opportunity to use his skills and experience for humanitarian ends, in keeping with his Quaker faith. He masterminded the effort to feed Belgians trapped by the German occupation of their country, and after the war he led the United States's mission to send food and supplies to Europe's stricken people. He achieved extraordinary success in both endeavors and became famous for his public service.

Buttoned-up and reserved, Hoover wasn't much of a politician. After a feeble attempt to win the Republican nomination in 1920, he joined President Warren G. Harding's cabinet as secretary of commerce. He remained in this position for eight years and made it into a far more important post than it had traditionally been. As secretary, he cultivated an image of the selfless technocrat, a starched-collar administrator interested mainly in making government and the economy more efficient, while sticking to the traditional, small-town values that had made him who he was. In 1928, he parlayed his prominence in the Harding and Coolidge administrations into the Republican nomination for president. He had never held elective office.[2]

On the surface, Al Smith couldn't have been more different. Instead of starched collars and dark business suits, he wore showy hats and jackets, a huge cigar tucked in the corner of his mouth. He flaunted his New York accent and boasted that his alma mater wasn't MIT, but FFM—the Fulton Fish Market. The historian Alan J. Lichtman called him "a true New York provincial."[3]

Smith was as voluble as Hoover was reserved. The New Yorker loved to hold court, entertain, and banter with his friends. Although he called himself an immigrant, his family had come to the United States three decades before his birth.

His forebears hailed from Ireland and Italy, and they achieved a modest success—at least for his Lower East Side neighborhood, 60 percent of whose inhabitants were foreign-born. The neighborhood, now known as Two Bridges for its proximity to the Brooklyn and Manhattan Bridges, was one of the densest in New York, packed with tenements in "bad sanitary condition."[4]

Outwardly, Smith's life on the immigrant streets of New York seemed the polar opposite of Hoover's in his tiny Iowa town, population 501 in 1880. But both men had strict religious upbringings, learning the values of individual responsibility, hard work, and Victorian morality. Smith's early biographers compared the inhabitants of his parish with "the people of the Middle West": for both, "virtue was virtue, vice was vice. The ideas of the parents did not differ profoundly from the children's [and] everybody worked, and everybody took work for granted."[5]

Like Hoover, Smith lost both his parents as a young boy, and he quit school at age thirteen to support himself and his siblings. He got a job as a clerk for a wholesale fish dealer and acted in a local theater group on the side. In his passion for acting, he differed profoundly from Hoover, who was always uncomfortable center stage. Smith loved attention and adulation; if he couldn't make a living in the theater, he would turn to politics as an alternative way to reward his talents.

On the Lower East Side, Tammany Hall was the only game in town, and Smith quickly worked his way up through the Democratic machine—all the while remaining largely unsullied by it. He was elected to the state assembly in 1903 and became the body's Democratic leader a decade later. He developed a reputation as a reformer, eager to improve the lives of the poor and the working class. After serving as sheriff of New

York County, he won the first of his four terms as governor of New York. As the state's chief executive, Smith pushed the legislature to improve factory safety, protect women and children workers, build low-cost housing, improve public education, and create a network of parks.[6] The governor worked closely with Robert Moses, the great architect of parks, roadways, and recreation facilities for New York City and Long Island and, in the 1920s, still associated with progressive politics.[7] But despite Smith's legislative accomplishments, his greatest successes came in his effort to make government more efficient—just like Herbert Hoover.

If Hoover was best known as a skillful manager, Smith disguised his bureaucratic prowess beneath a man-of-the-people personality. To immigrants, Smith represented the promise of the American dream, the ability to rise to the top without leaving his origins behind. This persona made him a hero of urban immigrant groups but an anathema in much of the rest of the country. Smith's opposition to Prohibition allowed opponents to label him as immoral and his working-class demeanor as uncouth. Above all, it was his Catholicism that made him unacceptable to the majority of Americans.

In 1928, most native-born white Protestants from small towns and rural areas supported Prohibition and were susceptible to anti-Catholic and anti-Jewish messages. They also worried that big-city politicians didn't understand them.[8] During the electoral campaign, those religious messages were intense, although they came mostly from outside Hoover's entourage, whose members nonetheless encouraged them quietly. The main sources of anti-Catholic hostility and paranoia, which commonly dovetailed with the defense of Prohibition and fear of immigrants, were Protestant ministers and journalists, local politicians, school-board members, small-town newspapers, and, of course, the Ku Klux Klan, revived for the 1928 election.

Even before Smith's nomination, the *Atlantic Monthly* ran a piece by Charles C. Marshall, a Protestant expert on canon law, that raised doubts about Smith's fitness for the presidency. Wouldn't the Catholic Smith owe his primary allegiance to the pope? "There is a note of doubt," Marshall wrote, "a sinister accent of interrogation, not as to [Smith's] intentional rectitude and moral purpose, but as to certain conceptions [that] are irreconcilable with that Constitution which as President you must support and defend, and with the principles of civil and religious liberty on which American institutions are based." Marshall proceeded to cite papal bulls and other Catholic texts to show, quoting the *Catholic Encyclopedia*, that the Roman Catholic Church "regards dogmatic intolerance, not alone as her incontestable right, but as her sacred duty." In other words, to be a Catholic is, by definition, to deny the religious pluralism and religious freedom so dear to American life. Worse, Catholic doctrine "inevitably makes the Roman Catholic Church at times sovereign and paramount over the State." As for the pope, the Catholic Church claims that his authority "is not only superior in theory to the sovereignty of the secular State, but is substituted upon earth in place of the authority of God himself." Marshall concluded by challenging Smith to show that his concerns were unwarranted and that the "citizens who hesitate in their endorsement of your candidacy because of the religious issues involved" should not withhold their votes.[9]

Marshall's essay was almost unreadably scholarly in tone, and it represented a gentle, apparently respectful, version of the anti-Catholicism that would mark the presidential campaign. Smith was unfamiliar with the armature of citations that supported the piece, and he confessed to being unable to read it.[10] He didn't want to respond, but his top advisors, Belle Moskowitz and Joseph Proskauer, both Jewish, convinced him that he had to. After consulting a leading Catholic theologian, they drafted a point-by-point critique of Marshall's essay to be published under Smith's name. The text declared that "no power in the institution of my Church" could ever "interfere with the operation of the Constitution of the United States." It ended with "a fervent prayer that never again in this land will any public servant be challenged because of the faith in which he has tried to walk humbly with his God."[11]

Smith won the rhetorical battle, at least for the elite readers of the *Atlantic Monthly*, but Marshall's essay gave a measure of intellectual respectability to a pair of notions that would dog the governor's campaign and damage his candidacy for president: that his primary loyalty would be to the pope, not the American people, and that because the pope was an absolutist ruler who demanded subservience, a Catholic like Smith could never understand or respect the principles of American democracy.[12]

The typical anti-Catholic, anti-Smith screed would never have been published in the *Atlantic Monthly*; the more hotly prejudiced writings circulated in a variety of lowbrow Protestant newspapers, pamphlets, handbills, cartoons, and the like. They included a pamphlet by Robert Schuler, a Los Angeles minister, who declared, "Al Smith is distinctly Rome's candidacy. . . . If America desires a President born and raised in a foreign atmosphere . . . that man may be had by electing Al Smith."[13] Another cleric, Dr. Mordecai Cam, pastor of Oklahoma City's largest Baptist church, told his congregation, "If you vote for Al Smith you're voting against Christ, and you'll all be damned."[14]

A drumbeat of anti-Smith invective came from the *Christian Advocate*, a Methodist paper and one of the oldest journals in the United States. In that paper, Bishop James Cannon, a leader of the Prohibitionist Anti-Saloon League, called the Catholic Church the "mother of ignorance, superstition, intolerance and vice."[15] In Atlanta, a group of Protestant ministers announced its opposition to Smith, saying, "You cannot nail us to a Roman cross and submerge us in a sea of rum." A Baptist pastor from Texas maintained that Catholics weren't Christian, while the *Christian Century*, America's top Protestant magazine, wrote in opposing Smith that they could not "look with unconcern upon the seating of a representative of an alien culture, of a medieval Latin mentality, of an undemocratic hierarchy and of a foreign potentate in the great office of President of the United States."[16]

Hoover refused to make religiously biased statements himself, but he didn't forcefully denounce religious bigotry until late in the campaign. There is evidence, Lichtman writes, that the leadership of the Republican Party deliberately, if covertly, exploited the widespread Protestant hostility to the possibility of a Catholic president. In one prominent case, a Republican official wasn't so covert. Mabel Walker Willebrandt, the assistant attorney general for Prohibition enforcement, spoke to dozens of Protestant church groups urging them to have parishioners vote against Smith. Willebrandt didn't openly attack the governor's Catholicism, but his religion was the clear subtext beneath her denunciations of Smith for flouting Prohibition and supposedly consorting with bootleggers, gangsters, and other unsavory characters.[17]

Franklin Delano Roosevelt, the Democratic candidate to replace Smith as New York governor, received stacks of letters from random correspondents excoriating the Democratic presidential candidate. Shortly after Labor Day, one correspondent wrote that "if Gov. Smith is elected President, the Pope' son [*sic*] will be his secretary." Another told FDR that Catholicism's "sacred book of rules" requires believers "to tear out the womb of any Protestant woman—For by so doing you abolish the perpetuity of that Satanic following."[18] Letters sent to Roosevelt after the election mostly cited religion or Prohibition, or both, as the reasons for opposing Smith. Religion came out on top with 55.5 percent of the mentions, followed by Prohibition with 33 percent. Prohibition, of course, dovetailed with religion, as Protestants mostly supported it and Catholics didn't.[19]

Also closely related to religion was immigration, which had brought large numbers of Catholics—and to a lesser, but significant, extent, Jews—to the United States. At the beginning of the electoral campaign, an editorial in the *Baltimore Sun* claimed that a President Smith would mean the "unloosing on us [of] a horde of immigrants from such races as have already been proved hardest to assimilate. It is plain that the object of this is to increase the foreign vote in the cities, which can be depended on to vote for liquor and be easily controlled by machines."[20] A similar statement came from the president of the Kiwanis Club in Clarkson, Tennessee, who declared, "prior to [the 1890s], the overwhelming majority of entrants [to the United States] were of a racial stock akin to our own." But now, "the inflow has been of a distinctly different and decidedly inferior character,

Italians, southern Slovenes, Magyars . . . the very antithesis of the Anglo-Saxons." The Baptist minister A. J. Barton added that "the greatest issue in this campaign [is] whether we shall continue our American civilization or lower it to the standards" of the incoming mob of Catholics and Jews.[21] Since Smith represented and embodied these inferior hordes, he had to be stopped at all costs.

Among the anti-Smith voices, the Ku Klux Klan was consistently the most extreme, although its statements often mirrored those of more mainstream groups. By 1928, the Klan had been in decline for three years, but the election temporarily revived its fortunes.[22] A reinvigorated hooded order blanketed the country with anti-Smith pamphlets, newspapers, and images by the millions. Its national paper, the *Fellowship Forum*, declared early on that "the real issue in this campaign [is] Protestant Americanism versus rum and Romanism." Under a Smith presidency, "America becomes a vassal state of the Vatican and a stink-slide of booze and corruption." The voters will have to decide, the editors added, whether "to remain a Nation of thoroughbred Americans or to be turned into a dumping ground of the scum of Europe and Asia."[23] A flyer for a Klan-sponsored book on the horrors of Catholicism exclaimed, "Will it come to this?" It showed an image of priests burning a baby alive and burning a Protestant woman at the stake. Depicted as well were several Protestants hanging from a tree, recalling the St. Bartholomew Day's Massacre in sixteenth-century France, when thousands of Calvinists were strung up.[24]

Roosevelt estimated that the *Fellowship Forum* spent between two and four million dollars on printing and postage during the campaign. The expenditures paid off: according to FDR, the paper had insinuated itself into even tiny villages such as his own Hyde Park. The KKK had indeed reappeared throughout New York State, especially Buffalo, Syracuse, and Albany.[25]

The Klan also staked out a significant presence in Massena. Stanley Cappiello, who was a teenager in 1928, remembered seeing a huge number of flyers advertising the KKK's upcoming meetings in the village, and Klansmen had handed him literature saying, among other things, that if Smith were elected, the pope would move to Washington, D.C. Cappiello saw several cross burnings as well: "On a rise about one-fourth of a mile from my parents' property," he wrote, "was the location the Klan used to burn crosses. I saw at least 10 crosses burned from the spot [and] white robed people moving around in the lit-up area of the burning cross." He also witnessed cross burnings behind Kauffman's Department Store. The Klan had picked the location not only because of its proximity to the Jewish shop but also because a Catholic man running for local office lived nearby. A news article in the *Massena Observer* confirms Cappiello's recollections.[26]

So do other local newspapers, which reported a fair amount of Ku Klux Klan activity in the area. As the presidential campaign was getting underway in September 1928, the Ogdensburg *Republican-Journal* wrote, "A large number of local people attended a meeting of the Ku Klux Klan" in a rural area about thirty miles from Massena. They came in "several hundred cars," and their vehicles "formed an open air arena and with their lights played on the center, made an imposing bright spot in the pitch darkness."[27] At about the same time, "a state official of the Klan" held a meeting in Gouverneur to explain the "relationship of the Klan to American institutions."[28] Another Klan

The Ku Klux Klan burned crosses in Massena in 1928.

gathering took place in Macomb (35 miles from Massena) in late September, and yet another brought together 125 people in the same village a few weeks later.[29]

These reports of Klan activity in and around Massena don't identify the members, so we can't be certain that Massena firefighters belonged to the organization, as many of the town's residents alleged at the time of the blood libel. But it's plausible that this was the case and also that the presence of the hooded order heightened tensions during the electoral campaign. Given the religious hostilities enflamed by the KKK, members of the organization who helped with the search for Barbara Griffiths might have spread the rumor of Jewish ritual murder, even if they didn't necessarily originate it.

In any case, Klan activity in Massena was extensive enough for the synagogue president Jake Shulkin and his son Sam to attend a meeting out of curiosity. The two Jews declared themselves shocked both by the number of people attending the meeting and by their apparent acceptance of the Klan ideology. The Shulkins noted the presence at the meeting of members of the town's Volunteer Fire Department.[30]

The Shulkins and other Massena residents, like millions of others around the country, would have heard plenty of violent anti-Smith propaganda. After the Democratic convention nominated Smith in June, *The Railsplitter*, one of the KKK's many publications, declared, "The anti-Christ has won."[31] A few weeks later, the Klan secretary in Bay Shore, Long Island, said of the election: "This fight is not only a battle against Rome, but against all the evil forces in America: cutthroats, thugs, the scum from the cesspools of Europe."[32] In yet another Klan publication, *Heroes of the Fiery Cross*, Bishop Alma White supplied even more details about the enemies, represented by Smith, of the "one hundred percent Americans": "bootleggers . . . white slavers, toe-kissers, wafer-worshippers," and especially "the great Hebrew syndicates that have acquired a monopoly of the motion picture industry." These Jews, like all Jews, were "conscienceless, money-mad" people with "no worthy ideals, either of dramatic art or virtue." They "are destroying the moral standards of America and educating our youths in vice."[33]

Beyond Catholicism and Judaism, the generalized evil that Smith represented, encouraged, and embodied became a key KKK theme. For the New Yorker John Roach Straton, a leading Klan orator, the Democratic candidate epitomized everything that was wrong with American culture and society: "card-playing, cocktail drinking, poodle dogs, divorces, novels, stuffy rooms, dancing, evolution, Clarence Darrow, overeating, nude art, prize fighting, actors, greyhound racing, and modernism."[34] The final word in this list summed up the problem: Al Smith represented modern life, and modernity was the enemy of a traditional, "one hundred percent American" America under threat.

For all the religious bigotry associated with the Republican campaign of 1928, the GOP was not alone in mobilizing prejudice for political ends. Since Reconstruction, the South had voted solidly Democratic, and to maintain that largely white support, the Smith campaign kept African Americans at arm's length—or worse. At the Democratic convention in Houston, the first such gathering held in the South since the Civil War, black delegates were forced to sit inside a wire cage, walled off from the white delegates. Although Smith himself seemed to harbor little prejudice against blacks, his campaign took pains to reassure white southern voters that a Smith administration would do nothing to disrupt the racial hierarchy in the South. Southern Democratic leaders who supported Smith went considerably further. "Yes, Smith is a Tammany man, a Catholic, and a wet," argued one Democratic politician, "but wouldn't you rather have him in the White House than a President who compels white men and women to associate with negroes?" The bottom line, according to another southern Democratic official: "If you believe in White Supremacy, Vote the Straight Democratic Ticket."[35]

Despite such blatant appeals to Jim Crow, several of the country's black-owned newspapers lent Smith their support. Most prominent among them was the Chicago *Defender*, the nation's best-selling African American paper. Although blacks had traditionally backed Republicans, the Klan's virulent opposition to Smith evoked sympathy for him: his enemy was the enemy of African Americans. The same was true of a great many American Jews, put off by the Republicans' religious prejudice and hostility to recent immigrants, a category to which a large number of Jews belonged.[36] Given the nature of the campaign, Catholics appeared much more favorable to religious tolerance than Protestants, which disposed Jews, as victims of religious discrimination and hatred, to vote for Smith.

In Massena and upstate New York in general, Smith enjoyed little support; he had become governor thanks to the huge Democratic electorate of New York City.[37] As the *Massena Observer*, the town's ardently Republican newspaper, put it, "The Governor . . . is essentially the representative of those who throng the subways, crowd the market places, of those who dance in more or less happiness upon the Sidewalks of New York [the theme song of his campaign]. He stands for the aspirations of the clamorous cities, for the 'liberalism,' which these cosmopolitan centers desire. . . . He has been the choice of the great city; never of the broad acres."[38]

The *Massena Observer* believed, for good reason, that the overwhelming majority of the town's eligible voters would go for Hoover. Repeatedly, the paper's editorials explained to its readers how to register, where to register, and where to vote, and it urged them to cast their ballots on election day. The paper reported that, by the eve of the election, 3,555 Massenans, representing 100 percent of eligible voters, had registered. This number is virtually identical to the native-born population of the village age twenty-one and above, the legal voting age at the time.[39] Massena's electorate was thus almost exclusively white (there were 15 African Americans age twenty-one and up) and native-born, precisely the group, outside the Deep South, that voted overwhelmingly Republican. Massena's large immigrant population may have favored Al Smith, but, as noncitizens, they couldn't vote for him. When my great-grandfather Jesse Kauffman became an American citizen in 1900, he was one of just six Democrats in the entire town of Massena.[40]

Despite the overwhelmingly Republican traditions of the upstate region, the *Massena Observer*, like other local papers, left nothing to chance; most observers understood that Smith had no path to the presidency without New York State's electoral votes. "No one can afford to stay away from the polls this year," the *Observer* proclaimed, for "there have been more elections lost by voters staying away while the opposition crept into power than in any other way. Your vote may be the one necessary to make the majority."[41]

In urging Massenans to vote, the *Observer*'s editors were not above mobilizing racial and religious stereotypes. Reporting on a well-received speech Smith had given in Missouri, the *Observer* wrote, "great was the applause . . . but applause in Missouri means a half dozen white people enthusiastically cheering, about a hundred negroes following suit and a refrain to be taken up by the large number of jackasses which have made the state famous." As for Smith's core electorate, it featured, the *Observer* maintained, "that large class of people who find themselves almost broke preceding election time and that think if the administration was put in the hands of the opposite party, everything would turn out all right."[42] Others likely to choose Smith were those who equated "Al Smith and Al Cohol . . . the catch words of the Democratic campaign."[43]

In making such claims, the *Observer,* like its small-town counterparts, expressed confidence and concern all at once—confidence because of the country's great prosperity in 1928, but worry because of Smith's string of successful campaigns in New York State. There were no public opinion polls in 1928, so journalists and ordinary citizens alike had nothing but anecdotal evidence to buoy them. Many Hoover supporters took solace in the prospective vote of women, expected to turn out in large numbers for the first time since winning the suffrage battle eight years earlier. "The women are as intensely interested as the men, perhaps more so," wrote the *Potsdam Courier & Freeman,* published in Massena's neighboring village. Women, "can never be convinced that this nation needs either liquor or Tammany to keep its home fires burning."[44]

Smith's ties to Tammany Hall appeared as a mantra in the upstate New York press, suggesting not just that the Democratic candidate was corrupt but that he was not one of "us." The Potsdam *Herald-Recorder* ran a full-page advertisement headlined, "Let's Keep the Tammany Tiger out of the White House!" It pictured a ferocious tiger smashing its paws into the classical columns of the White House facade and quoted a recent *New York Times* editorial: "Tammany Hall . . . professes to cherish the people but at heart it always intends to exploit and debauch them." For good measure, the ad brought in the great Democratic tribune William Jennings Bryan, who called Tammany "a predatory band more interested in personal plunder than in party principle—a stench in the nostrils of decent Democracy, selfish, disloyal and corrupt."[45] At about the same time, the neighboring Canton *Commercial Advertiser* asked: "Do we want quack legislation, the corner saloon and a low competitive tariff—a government administered by those 'great and kindly men of 145 East 14th Street'?" the headquarters of Tammany Hall.[46] That Al Smith had kept Tammany at arms' length for decades went unmentioned.

To seal its case against Smith, the Potsdam paper asked, "Why change our present condition with its wonderful promise for the future just because Tammany Hall wants a finger in the pie? Why compromise the future of the home and family because a group of noisy wets think that booze is the greatest benefit to the people?" Smith's election, the editors added, "will unquestionably shake the present structure of our stability and prosperity to its very foundation."[47] Virtually no one foresaw the brutal irony of these words: less than a year later the "great prosperity" would give way to the Great Depression.[48]

The Potsdam paper's endorsement of Hoover and prosperity reiterated the editorial views of the *Massena Observer* and virtually every other journal published in the surrounding towns and villages of St. Lawrence County, none of which breathed a word about the anti-Catholic sentiments prominent among Hoover's supporters. The lone outlier in this raft of Republican papers was the *Ogdensburg Advance and St. Lawrence Sunday Democrat*, which ardently supported Smith. In the middle of the campaign, the *Advance* published a front-page article about a top New York City Episcopalian official, Ralph Adams Cram, who professed to be so appalled by the religious bigotry of the Republican campaign that he sided with Smith. Cram portrayed himself as "another of those who, though not Roman Catholics, are nevertheless Americans and are outraged by this recrudescence of blatant bigotry." Cram added that "many who would otherwise have voted for Mr. Hoover are so sickened by the present agitation and appalled by its implication that they will vote for Mr. Smith even though they may be unsympathetic with certain of his views." He meant, in particular, the Eighteenth (Prohibition) Amendment but believed that supporters of Prohibition would vote for Smith because the Republicans "threaten whatever we have left of civil and religious liberty." Cram's conclusion: "the greatest danger to the Republic is neither capitalism nor the trades unions; neither party tyranny nor Communism; not even materialism nor the license and the wildness of the younger generation. It is quite simply the threatened and complete control of government and society by the body of ignorance, prejudice and superstition" embedded in Hoover's Republican Party.[49]

Beyond reports such as this, the Democratic paper gave extensive coverage to the anti-Catholic "whispering campaign" coming from Hoover's local supporters while criticizing them for questioning the Democratic candidate's Americanness. The paper cited a Potsdam speech by the Reverend C. H. McVey, who called Governor Smith "the exponent of the ideals of the foreigner that seek to subvert and destroy what Americans hold most dear."[50] As the election approached, it quoted Smith's denunciations of the Republicans for having "enlisted the aid of organized bodies which are not in line with the principles of this great country, and I name here and now the Ku Klux Klan."[51]

With these reports, the Democratic paper echoed the Catholic daily published in Rochester, which, after New York City, housed the state's largest Catholic population. The *Rochester Catholic* condemned Hoover as "the candidate who will profit the most by the Klan, the Anti-Saloon League, the whispering bigots and the snobs," which is why, the editors said, the Republican candidate "has not repudiated them in such vigorous terms as to convince the public that he repudiates such support." Why such hostility to Catholicism? The answer, according to the *Rochester Catholic*, was that "the Protestant church in the United States has existed upon the unestablished fact that this is a Protestant country" and that a Catholic president would put an end to the Protestants' unmerited monopoly of power.[52]

If the newspapers of upstate New York, like their counterparts nationwide, were sharply divided by political sympathy and affiliation, they stood united over one crucial phenomenon: the unprecedented role and influence of radio in the 1928 presidential election. The *Gouverneur Free Press* complained that the wireless had destroyed face-to-face campaigning, especially in out-of-the-way places like St. Lawrence County, New York. "Wouldn't it be a lot of fun," the editors asked, "to have just one or two old time campaigners hit town . . . and go for each other's throats?" "This radio world has killed all that sort of fun."[53] Meanwhile, the Ogdensburg *Republican-Journal* lamented the strangeness, at campaign's end, of a valedictory address by Smith, a candidate known for his rousing, crowd-pleasing speeches, "prepared for delivery through the microphone to an unseen audience."[54] As for the Canton *Commercial Advertiser*, it noted with neither regret nor enthusiasm the turning of a historical page. "The political campaign just closed," the editors wrote, "was far different from any campaign previously fought out in this country." The difference didn't relate to the issues or the candidates involved but resided "in the intimate manner in which the wireless enabled millions of people to listen for weeks to the addresses of the candidates and other speakers of marked ability." If any voters failed to understand the issues featured in this election, they would have only themselves to blame. Voters, the editors added, would have no basis for claiming ignorance of the issues and candidates, since the radio had exposed them to both nonstop. This, of course, is a naive view of the mass media, but understandable perhaps since this was the first election in American history in which millions of people could hear the actual voices of the candidates.

For the previous presidential election in 1924, the United States counted just 24 radio broadcasting stations. By 1928, the number of stations had soared to 763, including two nationwide networks, the National Broadcasting Company (NBC) and the Columbia Broadcasting System (CBS), each of which linked individual stations via telephone lines.[55] Republicans and Democrats not only depended on radio to broadcast political speeches but also used it to advertise their candidates and platforms and to criticize their opponents. Such advertising over the airwaves constituted a first in American politics.[56]

By 1928, more than 50 percent of U.S. households owned radios, representing a potential audience of more than 40 million listeners for the two parties. And the public seemed mesmerized by the new technology. The Democratic Party received some 250,000 letters and 10,000 telegrams in response to its political programming, and the Republicans registered 100,000 letters and telegrams, many of which contained, or promised, significant financial contributions.[57]

The candidates, however, took a while to get used to the new medium. Hoover tended to look down at his feet while he spoke, causing the era's primitive microphones to miss many of his words and produce unintelligible gaps in his speech. As for Smith, he was such a frenzied orator, flailing, weaving, and bobbing as he spoke, that his words either exploded into the microphone or missed it altogether. The radio also tended to exaggerate his New York City accent, which boosted the Republicans' portrayal of him as "foreign" and out of touch with ordinary Americans. On the eve of the election, Hoover and Smith each spoke for an hour on nationwide radio, potentially reaching about one-third of the American public, or more than 40 million people. Until then, the record audience for any lone individual belonged to Dwight L. Moody, an evangelist believed to have spoken to 100,000 people—in his entire lifetime.[58]

Commentators at the time generally believed that, with network radio, politicians would no longer be able to say one thing to an East Coast audience and something else to a West Coast one. This notion overlooked the purely local stations, which retained far more influence in 1928 than the two national networks. Broadcasters also maintained that "radio will purify politicians" and that "religious intolerance cannot pass." But, if anything, the election of 1928 revealed far more religious intolerance than the American norm.[59]

What impressed the local upstate New York papers perhaps

more than anything was the radio's ability to transmit the election results with unprecedented speed. After the polls closed on election night, the various wire services would telegraph the vote totals in each locality to NBC, which would then broadcast them from their studios in New York, with regular interruptions to permit local stations to announce outcomes in their regions. "The large staff of political experts," wrote the *Ogdensburg Advance*, "will be in charge of news dissemination by the National Broadcasting Company," whose "program will be interspersed with a gala presentation of music and other entertainment by popular artists."[60]

Because the results would trickle in, NBC needed entertainers to keep its vast audience engaged. Still, an editorialist for the Ogdensburg *Republican-Journal* marveled over the technology involved. In many places, newfangled voting machines would, for the first time, record the ballots, after which "experienced men" would use "mechanical tabulators" to aggregate the results. They would then "flash" them to "one nerve center where the whole mass of figures is digested." By midnight, the presidential results would be known nationwide, barring an exceptionally tight race. Since the polls generally closed at 8 P.M., to know the winner within four hours seemed nothing short of remarkable.[61]

Chapter 6

A NATIONAL AFFAIR

At the time of Barbara Griffiths's disappearance, the presidential election campaign was about two weeks old. Her absence and the extensive, 300-person, round-the-clock search to find her put the campaign in St. Lawrence County on hold. Even so, the religious passions it had aroused played no small role in the unprecedented accusation against a group of small-town American Jews.

Following the early afternoon interrogation of Rabbi Brennglass on Sunday, September 23, nothing was resolved. Members of Massena's Jewish community, huddled in the synagogue, feared that something terrible would happen. It didn't help that the rabbi had had to wade through a crowd of 200 to 300 people, some of them hostile, as he walked to Adath Israel after his disturbing interview with the mayor and the police. Meanwhile, Barbara's parents, along with Massena's police officers, firefighters, and many other residents of the town, faced the mounting possibility that the four-year-old, missing now for twenty-four hours, was dead.

Believing perhaps that Barbara was gone, and that Massena's Jews would face dangerous repercussions, as had European Jews under similar circumstances, Shulkin, the synagogue president, redoubled his efforts to alert national Jewish leaders in New York City. Shortly after his hour-long telephone call to Louis Marshall, president of the American Jewish Committee, Shulkin contacted Rabbi Stephen Wise, who led the other national organization representing American Jews, the American Jewish Congress. It's unclear why Shulkin wrote to Wise after having made his urgent, long-distance call to Marshall just a few hours after Barbara Griffiths had gone missing. All we know of the call is that it resulted in Marshall's promise to send the journalist Boris Smolar to Massena as his representative.

Did Shulkin and Massena's other Jewish leaders consider Marshall's response too tepid? What Smolar wrote many years later suggests as much: "Marshall, not wanting to involve the American Jewish Committee before the full facts were established . . . asked me to urgently proceed to Massena to investigate the situation." Smolar added that "Marshall preferred not to alert the general press directly."[1] Always the careful, judicious attorney, Marshall seemed in no hurry to publicize the Massena story. Nor, it seems, was Smolar. Although he claimed fifty years later that he had hopped on a train and arrived in Massena midafternoon on Sunday—that is, the day after Barbara's disappearance—Smolar did not, in fact, reach Massena until Friday, September 28, six days after the call to Marshall.[2]

Hence, perhaps, Shulkin's letter to Wise on September 25

and Wise's immediate, telegraphed response.[3] What Shulkin didn't know was that by appealing to Marshall and Wise at the same time, he had unwittingly blundered into the long-standing rivalry between the two Jewish leaders. Marshall was a generally cautious Republican attorney, while Wise had distinguished himself as a fiery religious leader, a liberal Democrat, and a friend of Al Smith.

Marshall's American Jewish Committee (AJC), founded in 1906, emerged as the first organization in United States history created by an ethnoreligious group to defend the rights and interests of that group.[4] The organization's founders consisted mainly of well-to-do German Jews—lawyers, bankers, businessmen—who inhabited the comfortable Midtown and Upper East Side quarters of New York City. Their original goal was to help integrate into American society the huge number

Louis Marshall, president, American Jewish Committee

of mostly poor and ill-educated recent Jewish immigrants from
Eastern Europe. It was a paternalistic organization, at least in
its early phase, and it evoked great resentment from the poorer,
Lower East Side Jews it claimed to represent—mostly without
allowing those downtown Jews to represent themselves.

The AJC's leaders tended to be probusiness conservatives and
Republicans, who worked cautiously and quietly in an effort to
avoid hostile reactions from the Gentile establishment. Even so,
Marshall would find that his enthusiastic support for continued
Jewish immigration put him sharply at odds with Gentile conservatives eager to close the door to Ellis Island. His defense
of immigrants' rights launched him down the road to social
reform, both in the United States and abroad. He came to the
defense of Jews facing oppression overseas, and in this country
he supported the NAACP and litigated on its behalf. He also
advocated for the rights of Native Americans and became an
ardent environmentalist before the term had even been coined.[5]

Despite Marshall's advocacy of immigrants' rights and the
rights of different minority groups, his AJC couldn't shake its
top-down, paternalistic lineage. At the end of the First World
War, a rival Jewish organization, the American Jewish Congress, took shape. The Congress, long dominated by Stephen
Wise, cast itself as a democratic counterweight to the AJC. It
gave representation to the poorer Jews who had come from Russia and Eastern Europe and became an ardently Zionist organization in the wake of Britain's Balfour Declaration in 1917,
which "view[ed] with favor the establishment in Palestine of
a national home for the Jewish people." Marshall and the AJC
were agnostic, at most, about Zionism, but to the new American Jewish Congress, Zionism expressed the aspirations of the

world's struggling Jewish masses.[6] For Louis Brandeis, one of the Congress's founders, Jewish nationalism held out the same promise as the United States—a promise of freedom, "a movement to enable Jews to exercise the right now exercised by practically every other people in the world."[7]

While Shulkin waited for Marshall to take action in response to his urgent phone call, Barbara suddenly stumbled out of the woods, bewildered and disoriented but unharmed. At about 4:30 on Sunday afternoon, just over twenty-four hours after she had disappeared, the four-year-old was spotted in a farmer's field less than a mile from her house. Two teenage girls from the

Rabbi Stephen Wise, president,
American Jewish Congress

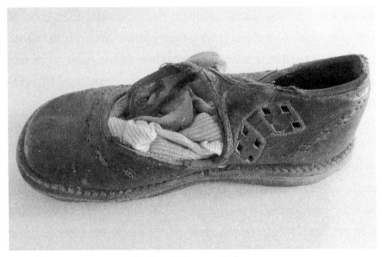

Barbara's damaged shoe

nearby village of Norfolk saw her as they waited by the roadside for a ride home. Fully aware of the drama in Massena, which "had spread through the entire county and beyond," the girls immediately realized that the little one must be Barbara. They flagged down a passing car, whose driver, also aware of the saga, took Barbara into his arms and drove her home.[8]

"Her clothing was somewhat torn," the *Observer* wrote, "and she was pretty tired and hungry, but otherwise none the worse for her experience." Barbara told her parents that after failing to find her brother the day before, she waded into some tall grass and soon lost her bearings. When darkness fell and the temperature dropped, she curled up in the grass to try to warm her bare legs, clad as she was in a light gingham dress. Shivering in the chilly autumn night—fall arrived early in the north country—she fell asleep.

When Barbara awakened in the sunlight on Sunday morning, her clothes were dripping wet—it had rained during the night. But they dried in the sun as she tried to find her way home. She didn't know in what direction to go, which is why several hours went by before she glimpsed a road in the distance and saw the two older girls, who helped her into a passing car and into the arms of her family. Overjoyed, Barbara's parents told the *Observer*, "we are aware of the hundreds of men who spent hours, both day and night, searching for our lost child [and] we want you to know that your efforts are appreciated by us." Dave Griffiths added, "In times of sorrow and need the people of Massena always respond to the occasion. They have done this for us."[9]

It took several hours for the news of Barbara's safe return to spread around the village, and perhaps 200 people continued to hunt for her until late Sunday night. After most of the searchers had returned to town, a rumor spread that the Jews, having kidnapped the child, decided to let her go after seeing how much the town had mobilized on her behalf.[10] It's unclear whether the Griffiths ever entertained the idea that the Jews had kidnapped or killed their daughter, but they didn't mention the accusation in their statements to the press. To escape the charged atmosphere in Massena, Barbara's mother fled with her two children to New York City.[11] For its part, the *Massena Observer* wrote only about Barbara's disappearance and return; it never breathed a word about the blood libel in its community. As for Barbara herself, she said ninety years later that, as a child and a teenager, she was commonly greeted with the refrain: "Oh, you're the girl who got lost in the woods."[12]

If the local Massena paper ignored the unprecedented American ritual murder accusation, the rest of the press, in upstate New York and throughout the United States, gave it elaborate coverage. By early October 1928, the Massena blood libel had been transformed from a strange local event to a huge national scandal. Two men played the key roles in nationalizing the Massena events: the Jewish leaders Marshall and Wise. Both intended to defend the Jews of Massena, to exact a measure of retribution against the Massena officials responsible for the blood libel, and ultimately to teach Americans a lesson about the damage antisemitism could do. Although Marshall quickly mobilized the machinery of the American Jewish Committee, it was Wise who acted most decisively.

The rabbi responded by telegram and mail immediately after receiving the letter Shulkin had sent him early on Tuesday, September 25, about thirty-six hours after Barbara's reappearance. Shulkin's letter told of the lost child, the accusation against the Jews of Massena, the interrogation of Rabbi Brennglass, and the young girl's safe return to her family. Shulkin concluded with a note of desperation: "We feel that we cannot drop this case. We are strong in our opinion that it is a *national affair*. We do not know how to proceed. We request that you immediately inform us what action to take."[13] The telegraphed response from Wise's secretary did just that: "DR WISE HAS WRITTEN [you a long letter] URGE YOU DEMAND FORMAL APOLOGY ALSO SECURE NAME SOCALLED FOREIGNER RESPONSIBLE SPREADING OUTRAGEOUS RUMOR."[14] In his letter, the Congress president assured Shulkin of his support and the complete backing of his organization: "This thing must be cleared up and cleared up immediately and fully. The Jewish members of your community and we shall not rest content until there be the most ample and unequivocal apology. It is tragic enough that the the [sic] term 'ritual murder' should be used in European lands of darkness. I do not propose to let this matter rest until there be the fullest explanation on the part of those responsible. . . . The honor of American Israel" is at stake.[15]

Wise's next step was to telephone Governor Al Smith, whom the Jewish leader had known and collaborated with for years. The rabbi asked Smith to make clear to the residents of Massena that the ritual murder accusation was beyond the pale and to discipline both Mayor Hawes and Trooper McCann. Shortly after the call to Smith's office, Wise wrote to Major John Warner, superintendent of the New York State Police and the governor's son-in-law, asking him to ensure "that the fullest amends . . . be made to the Jewish community of Massena and that nothing less than a most explicit apology will be satisfactory." Such actions are especially necessary, Wise added, because "the rumour is being broadcast that after questioning the Rabbi, the guilty [Jews] became frightened and gave up the child." (Wise meant, of course, "after the police questioned the rabbi, the guilty [Jews]. . . .") That is, the Jews supposedly decided not to kill the kidnapped girl for fear of being caught in the act. Wise also contacted Mayor Hawes, directing him to "do whatever may be necessary not merely to contradict the base rumour of ritual murder, but point out in addition that no intelligent, decent person has ever given any credence to this charge."[16]

Wise declined to publicize his calls and letters to state and local officials, because he didn't want the Massena incident to become a "national affair," as Shulkin had called it. In a note to his children, the rabbi said he had "kept the thing out of the English [language] press" because he didn't want the ritual murder charge to be aired in public, lest Americans hostile to Jews get dangerous ideas.[17] Marshall, however, preempted Wise— and contradicted his original, cautious, stance—by releasing his own detailed, three-page single-spaced letter about the case to the *New York Times*.

The letter, addressed to Mayor Hawes, exhibited none of the rhetorical restraint typical of the usually temperate Jewish leader. In hot language, Marshall declared Hawes responsible for "one of the most shocking exhibitions of bigotry that has ever occurred in this country." Hawes, "together with Corporal H.M. McCann of Troop B of the State police, were active participants in the outrage perpetrated." Marshall added, "what has occurred does not merely affect the Jews of Massena, whose very lives were placed in jeopardy, but the entire Jewish population of this country and of the world."

As the long letter went on, newspaper readers could hear the anger in Marshall's voice. He told Hawes, "your action might have resulted in one of those many calamities recorded on the bloody pages of medieval, and even modern European history." That Hawes could have entertained for one second the notion of Jewish ritual murder "is an abomination and betokens unfitness for public office." Had Barbara Griffiths not turned up unharmed, Hawes's "official irresponsibility" would have "culminated in mob violence." Marshall concluded by demanding a "public written apology to the Jewish people for . . . this wanton attack upon their religion and upon their honor." This apology

"must be couched in such terms as will meet with my approval."
If Hawes failed to give it, Marshall promised to "institute pro-
ceedings . . . for your removal from office."[18]

Now that the Massena incident had gone public, Wise
decided to air his own Massena interventions in the *New York
Times*. He began by dictating a statement to Al Smith's (Jewish) chief of staff, Belle Moskowitz—a condensed version of
which the governor's office released to the press. "As Governor
of the State," the dispatch read, "I cannot believe that this libelous myth has been resurrected and credited even for a moment
by any one [*sic*] connected with the service of the State. . . . I
can hardly believe that either the Mayor of Massena or a State
trooper summoned a rabbi to a police station on a religious holiday in connection with an absurd ritual murder charge." Smith
concluded by promising that "as Governor of the State of New
York . . . this matter will be investigated in the most thorough
manner."[19] In condensing the text Wise had dictated to her, Moskowitz left out the rabbi's strongest sentence: "There will be
no toleration of an attempt by any public official to give countenance to the grotesque accusation of ritual murder, or any
equally baseless indictment against a whole people . . . while I
am the Governor." Moskowitz added, as Wise had not, that the
governor has the authority to investigate the state trooper, but
not the mayor.[20]

When contacted by the *Times*, neither Hawes nor McCann
agreed to issue any statement, whether an apology or a defense.
But on October 2, Hawes wrote Wise with what amounts to a
justification of his actions. "The incident," Hawes wrote, "has
been enlarged and magnified and from the contents of your
letter I feel sure that you do not fully understand the facts. It

is not a matter that is being discussed in Massena and very few people know anything about it and if it gains publicity it will only be through the Jewish people of Massena." Hawes denied that he harbored "ill feeling against the Jewish people of this community" and claimed, "there is no local prejudice or hostility."[21] He appeared stung by Shulkin's unwillingness to accept the informal apology he had offered during a visit to Massena's synagogue a few days earlier. When Smolar, the journalist representing Marshall, asked Hawes for a written apology, the mayor refused.[22]

Hawes's refusal and justification of his actions in the wake of Barbara's disappearance frustrated Wise to no end; had Marshall seen Hawes's letter, he would have been incensed. To defuse the situation and keep it from exploding further in the press, Wise worked behind the scenes with Moskowitz and Warner to extract a written apology from Hawes and McCann. The stakes were high for several reasons. The Massena incident was the United States's first serious blood libel, and Wise sought reassurance for American Jews all too familiar with the violent consequences of ritual murder accusations in their former European homelands. Wise also wanted American Gentiles to understand the gravity of this antisemitic charge, coming as it did on the heels of Henry Ford's long anti-Jewish campaign and the revival of the Ku Klux Klan. But unlike Marshall, the rabbi thought the effort required delicate diplomacy: he wanted to reassure American Jews without sparking a backlash against them.

Wise also understood the potential consequences of the Massena incident for the presidential election underway. Smith was the clear underdog in this race, and he couldn't possibly win without New York State's forty-four electoral votes. The Jewish electorate, much of which had traditionally supported Republicans, was crucial for the Democratic candidate. To win their votes, the governor had to intervene decisively on their behalf. As for New York State's Republicans, they too were eager to quiet the Massena situation for fear of pushing Republican Jews toward Smith. There is some evidence that the state's Republican leadership forced Hawes to release an unequivocal apology.[23]

The mayor finally issued one after an all-day meeting in Albany that included the Massenans Shulkin, Brennglass, McCann, and Hawes, plus Major Warner, Wise, and George Gordon Battle, an attorney representing the American Jewish Congress. In a letter to his children, Wise took full credit for the favorable outcome of the meeting: "I . . . dictated the statement [of apology from Hawes] that you may have seen in the *Times* today. . . . Then I dictated another letter from him to Mr. Marshall . . . then a letter of apology from the State trooper to the rabbi; then a letter from the two Jews [Shulkin and Brennglass] to Marshall, pointing out that they want the thing stopped. . . . Finally I prepared with Warner his report to the Governor."[24] Wise enclosed a copy of Hawes's apology, with annotations scrawled around the margins: "This, dearest children, is a fine document," and he hoped Marshall wasn't "foolish enough" to reject it.

The statement Hawes signed admitted that he had "committed a serious error of judgment" and wanted "to express clearly and unequivocally . . . my deep and sincere regret that . . . I should have seemed to lend countenance, even for a moment, to what I ought to have known to have been a cruel libel [against] the Jewish people." The letter went on to acknowledge the suffering European Jews had endured from the "unthinkable charges" of ritual murder and affirming that he never should have allowed Rabbi Brennglass "to be interrogated with regard to the myth of ritual murder." In exchange for these admissions, Wise apparently agreed not to press for Hawes's resignation as mayor, allowing him to say, "I know that the citizenship of Massena, including its Jewish members, will not seek to dishonor me through removal from office because of an error of judgment which no one deplores more than I do."[25]

Wise enthused to his children about these "thrilling and Wonderful [sic]" results and proved considerably less diplomatic in private correspondence than in his negotiations with public figures. Although Wise found himself impressed with Rabbi Brennglass, "there is less to be said for the president of the congregation at Massena." As for Trooper McCann, he "is just a stupid Catholic . . . who permitted himself to become the tool of the Klan." The mayor had "a K.K.K. 'ponim' [face]," but he is "either afraid or sorry or both" and willing "to make any decent apology." He wouldn't "dream of acceding to Mr. Marshall's terms that he apologize and resign."

After the apologies were signed, Wise spent an hour with Al Smith, whom he found "just as jolly as though he had been elected last week, instead of about to get [walloped] in November." Wise saw the governor as sincerely troubled by the Massena incident, about which he nonetheless had a sense of humor: "He was screamingly funny in analyzing the whole situation" but turned serious when Marshall's efforts to exact a more abject apology came up. "If Mr. Marshall keeps this up," Smith declared, "he will make that man [Mayor Hawes] a victim and a hero, and the K.K.K. will send him to the Congress of the United States or make him Governor."[26]

Smith's comment, assuming Wise had reported it accurately, doubtless reflected the governor's exasperation over the relentless attacks raining down on him, attacks echoed in one Klan publication after another and reinforced by local Republican officials. Smith knew, of course, that the Klan was active in upstate New York, a Hoover stronghold, and the Massena episode seemed to him—as to Wise—to demonstrate the organization's ability to do harm. The hooded order didn't, by itself, produce the blood libel, but it would have seemed plausible to the governor that it had. Smith, after all, had just denounced the KKK in a much-publicized Oklahoma City speech condemning the so-called one hundred percent Americans for "breathing the spirit of hatred against millions of [their] fellow citizens" and for forgetting "the great principle that Jefferson stood for, the equality of man."[27] The Massena incident gave Smith yet another opportunity to resist bigotry, in this instance against Jews, but he had to act carefully in the fraught electoral situation of 1928. To eke out a victory in his home state, he needed to reassure its Jewish population without creating a backlash among Gentiles. Smith surely exaggerated Marshall's ability to trigger that backlash, but he was right to find counterproductive the AJC leader's persistence in pressing for an apology to his liking.

But Marshall was nothing if not persistent. He pushed Hawes to sign what he considered a more comprehensive apology, namely one that came from him. A year earlier, the AJC president had convinced Henry Ford to do just that, and Marshall may have decided that if he could get one of the most famous and powerful figures in the United States to submit to him, the lowly mayor of a small town should certainly do the same.

After receiving a letter from Hawes containing the apology Wise had written for him, Marshall rejected it as inadequate. In a letter to Hawes, the AJC leader "asked for an apology not only on behalf of the Jews of Massena, but of all Jews who were affected by the occurrences of which I complained." That apology "should be in such terms as would be approved by me." To help Hawes win that approval, Marshall enclosed "a draft of a document which I feel that I have a right to ask you to sign and return to me."[28]

Marshall was upset not only because Hawes had signed the apology Wise had written, but because Shulkin and Brennglass had accepted the apology as well. Worse, Marshall was furious that his rival, Wise, had presided over the meeting in Albany to work out a resolution to the Massena affair and that he had not been invited to participate. In a sharply worded letter to Shulkin, Marshall complained that the Adath Israel president had asked him "to represent the Jews of Massena. Yet you undertook without submission to me, to accept the apologies of the Mayor and the Corporal, disregarding the important condition that I had made in my letter to the Mayor that any apology that he might make should be in a form approved by me." His pride deeply wounded, Marshall chastised Shulkin and Brennglass for having "in a most cavalier manner practically dismisse[d] me from the case and decide[d] an important proposition which in no manner concerns you. I refer to the question as to what the attitude of the Jewish people as a whole should be toward this episode." Marshall persisted in demanding a more abject apology from Hawes, whom he considered "guilty of the most serious offense ever perpetrated in this country upon the Jewish people, infinitely worse than anything that Henry Ford ever did."[29]

It's extraordinary that Marshall said the Massena blood libel "in no manner concerns you," the Jews of Massena, although he conceded that Rabbi Brennglass handled the ritual murder accusation admirably well. It's startling as well that Marshall considered Mayor Hawes "infinitely worse than . . . Henry Ford." Shulkin and Brennglass were taken aback by Marshall's harsh response to the resolution brokered by Wise: "We are very much upset," Shulkin wrote, "over the fact that the action taken in Albany does not meet with your approval. . . . We thought that [it] would."[30] As for Brennglass, he told Marshall, "it grieved me and is still grieving me to think that with our action—which was so innocent—we caused displeasure to you. Believe me that we are absolutely blameless."[31] The two Massenans clearly had no idea about the rivalry between Marshall and Wise or about the extent to which partisan politics had entered into the Massena situation.

Smith and Wise were hostile to Marshall for his support of Hoover, and they worried that the AJC leader would enflame, rather than calm, the state's ethnoreligious antagonisms and cost the governor politically. Marshall, meanwhile, took a proprietary attitude toward the Massena case, as if he were the lawyer representing the libeled Jews, and deeply resented Wise for having stage-managed a resolution. Marshall clearly thought that any resolution should be up to him.

As for Shulkin and Brennglass, as well as the rest of Massena's tiny Jewish community, they feared the consequences of pushing Mayor Hawes too far. As Shulkin wrote, "there is considerable re-action and feeling against the Jewish people of Massena since this matter was started. I feel that its continuance will be very harmful not alone to the Jewish residents of Mas-

sena, but to all [Jews] in this section of the State." Shulkin and
Brennglass maintained "that Mayor Hawes has been sufficiently
punished and humiliated." They knew that Hawes had been
"receiving signed and unsigned threatening letters to him and
his family from various parts of United States [sic]" and worried
that "if the matter is continued it may have a very unfavorable
re-action upon our people."[32]

Julius Frank, a key Jewish leader in Ogdensburg, some forty
miles from Massena, corroborated Shulkin's fears. Having traveled to Massena, Frank "found the Mayor in a very upset condition, owing to the very large number of letters which he showed
me, and some of which I read, which were not alone most cruel,
but undignified, threatening and couching the most disgraceful
language. [They] came from all over the United States." Hawes
understood that "an error was made, but insists . . . that it was
unintentional on his part." His "best friends" growing up "were
mostly Jewish boys"—a statement certainly false, as Hawes was
raised in Tarrytown, New York, where there was just a handful of Jews, all strictly Orthodox and unlikely to associate with
Gentiles, even if Gentiles had been open to them.[33] Frank must
have been skeptical of Hawes's claim but, even so, appeared to
sympathize with him. The mayor "is desirous," Frank wrote,
"as are the Jewish people of Massena, to have the publicity dis-
continued." Hawes didn't want to sign the apology Marshall
had drafted for "fear of further publicity." But he would sign it,
Frank said, if Marshall agreed not to publish it.[34]

The Massena incident had already received massive publicity,
with articles about it appearing not only in the big New York City
papers—the *Times*, the *Herald Tribune*, and the *Sun*—but also in
dozens of local upstate newspapers and a variety of Jewish jour-

nals, both in English and in Yiddish. If the New York papers covered the incident first, the Massena blood libel quickly became a cause célèbre nationwide. Newspaper accounts appeared in the *Washington Post, Boston Globe, Chicago Tribune, Baltimore Sun, Los Angeles Times, Atlanta Constitution*, and numerous small local papers, a sample of which includes the *Bluefield Daily Telegraph* in West Virginia, the *Lincoln Nebraska State Journal*, the *Joplin Globe* in Missouri, the *Lebanon Daily News* in Pennsylvania, the *Thomasville Times-Enterprise* in Georgia, the *Gastonia Daily Gazette* in North Carolina, the *Ada Evening News* in Oklahoma, the *Bismarck Tribune* in North Dakota, the *Ogden Standard Examiner* in Utah, the *Brownsville Herald* in Texas, and the *Bakersfield Californian*. Many of upstate New York's local newspapers expressed amazement that events occurring in their commonly ignored region of the country had, as the *Gouverneur Free Press* put it, "taken on a nation-wide aspect." As the story unfolded, the editors added, it attracted "even more [interest] than it caused at the time of [Barbara's] disappearance."[35]

Newspapers in smaller cities and towns generally ran the daily dispatches from the Associated Press about the Massena case, but big-city papers had their own correspondents cover it. Smaller papers complemented their AP articles with locally written pieces and letters to the editor, most of them sympathetic to the Jews of Massena. The *Kingston (NY) Daily Freeman* published a front-page article summarizing a "plea for understanding" by the town's rabbi. Like other Jewish leaders, the rabbi found it "incredible and almost inconceivable that in this country, the crown of religious tolerance and human sympathy, intelligent people, men of official position and responsibility should even harbor the suspicion of accusing the Jew of ritual murder."[36] The *Gastonia Daily Gazette* ran a long letter from the local rabbi recounting the sorry history of the blood libel and deploring that it had happened in the United States.[37] And many papers published the strongly worded statement released by the Permanent Commission for Better Understanding Between Christians and Jews in America. Drafted in part by Stephen Wise, the statement "solemnly affirm[ed] that the blood accusation is a cruel and utterly baseless libel on Judaism; that there is no such custom, ceremony or ritual among Jews anywhere, no more than there is among Christians anywhere, and nothing in their traditions or literature, which calls for the use of human blood for any purpose."[38]

Although the extensive, nationwide press coverage was overwhelmingly sympathetic to Massena's Jews and unfavorable to the town's mayor and police, some of the headlines written locally for the AP stories bucked the national trend. The *Indiana (PA) Evening Gazette*'s headline read, "New York Jews After Scalp of Massena Mayor."[39] Still, that Hawes received baskets of hate mail—and precious few friendly letters—seems to confirm the general lack of sympathy for him in the national press and the widespread incredulity over the ritual murder charge.

After the demise of the *Dearborn Independent* in 1927, the United States had no significant antisemitic press, as Canada and most continental European countries did, and the paucity of prominent anti-Jewish voices in the late 1920s kept the notion of ritual murder from gaining any purchase in this country. The situation might have been different had the blood libel occurred a few years later, when Father Coughlin, the populist radio preacher, grasped Henry Ford's anti-Jewish baton. But Tom Watson's populist precedent in the Leo Frank case, when the anti-Jewish ritual murder accusation didn't come up, suggests a general American immunity to the blood libel. How different it was in Hungary, Bohemia, Germany, Russia, Romania, and Quebec where, after each blood libel, antisemitic newspapers gave widespread publicity to the accusations against the Jews. Anti-Jewish journalists created detailed narratives, themselves based on earlier cases, that appeared to bolster the accusations and give their readers an apparently coherent story to believe.

In the United States, the Ku Klux Klan's many publications fixated on the election of 1928 and the effort to defeat Al Smith; the denunciation of Jews seemed of lesser importance. Still, in places like northern New York State, where the hooded order was active, Jewish leaders feared, perhaps rightly, that if the attacks on Hawes persisted, the Klan could redirect its fire toward the Jews. After all, a significant number of Massena residents appeared to believe that Jews were capable of murdering a child for ritual purposes. Shulkin and Brennglass, like Wise and Smith, decided that the safest course of action was to stop while they were ahead and allow the Massena incident to disappear from the news—which it largely did by mid-October 1928.

To put the incident to rest, Wise issued a statement saying the affair had been resolved. "We had all hoped that the ghastly myth of Jewish ritual murder would never be revived in our country. Alas that this was not to be, [but] having been evoked, the ghost was most promptly and effectually laid." Most important, "the Mayor of Massena, now conscious of the enormity of the evil of the human sacrifice legend, has apologized in such unequivocal fashion as becomes a gentleman and public servant." Wise nodded to Al Smith for "the promptness and vigor with which the Governor of New York has handled the situation," an intervention that "ought to leave the Massena incident unique in American annals." We can be thankful, Wise concluded, that "the Massena incident is now closed—happily for Israelism and Christendom."[40]

Even Marshall seemed mollified by Hawes's offer to sign the apology he had written, provided it was kept out of the press. It helped, as well, that Major Warner had suspended Trooper McCann from the state police for "conduct unbecoming an officer."[41] In a telegram to Julius Frank, Marshall recalled that he had "quieted down the public after Henry Ford's apology," and he promised to do so again.[42] Still, Marshall was unwilling to completely let the matter go, writing several more letters to Warner complaining that he had disciplined Trooper McCann behind Marshall's back.

Several other Jewish leaders joined Marshall in refusing to endorse Wise's view that the Massena incident had been fully resolved. New York assemblyman Julius S. Berg, commander of the Jewish Veterans of the Wars of the Republic, declared that no apology would suffice and that if Hawes failed to resign as mayor, he should be removed from office.[43] The *Kansas City Jewish Chronicle*, meanwhile, condemned Wise for having intruded "in so unceremonious fashion in so delicate a matter" and "having made a mess of the Massena incident" by using the horror of the ritual murder accusation to serve the political ambitions of Rabbi Wise.[44]

If the Massena case faded by mid-October from the national press, it remained very much alive in a variety of Jewish periodicals. Some sided with Wise and others with Marshall, and each side justified the strategy and actions of its champion. Abraham Rosenthal of the St. Louis Jewish weekly, *The Modern View*, supported Marshall's effort to have Hawes fired, maintaining, "To let the official [Hawes] keep his place is to condone . . . bigotry and ignorance. . . . Such men must be eradicated and eliminated." Rosenthal doubtless didn't mean this literally, although the harsh words reveal just how much Jewish fears had been aroused. If Jews failed to join Marshall in making an example of Hawes, Rosenthal added, we will "turn backward from progress to the darker ages that we THOUGHT were left behind!"[45]

All told, Marshall received "many hundreds [of letters] on the Massena affair," most highly favorable toward the AJC president's handling of the case.[46] But one clipping included with the stack of letters harshly condemned what it called Marshall's autocratic behavior. American Jews, wrote an editorialist for Toronto's *Canadian Jewish Review*, lived under "Marshall law," a system in which the AJC president took "it for granted that any Jewish business is his business." And in the case of Massena, "the impression furnished was that the matter was between the Mayor of Massena and one, Mr. Marshall . . . anointed head of the Jewish people."[47]

The most bizarre letter to Marshall came from one David Diamond of Lincoln, Nebraska, who thought the Massena affair, which "electrified the whole United States," was "a Jesuit intrigue to boost Smith." Diamond said that because the Jews of New York held the keys to the presidential election, they alone could stymie the Jesuits by voting en masse for Hoover. Otherwise, "the Eighty Five Million protestants [*sic*] in the United States will blame the Jews for this election [of Smith]."[48] This not-so-veiled threat, which echoed those of the Ku Klux Klan, showed that the reverberations of the Massena blood libel sounded not just in New York State or the major coastal cities, but throughout the American heartland. In many ways, Massena distilled the intense religious and ideological conflicts of the 1928 election and, partly for that reason, became an event of national import.

Like Marshall, Wise received stacks of letters in the wake of the Massena affair, and unsurprisingly, most were favorable to him. Morris Marguilies sent "congratulations on the fine and successful method pursued in connection with the Massena affair" and mocked "his Majesty, Louis the Somewhat [Marshall]" for his "long legalistic letters in a State where 'Al' is His excellency the Governor."[49] As if to confirm what David Diamond had had to say, one of the most laudatory of Wise's correspondents was a Jesuit named Cornelius Clifford, who wrote from Our Lady of Mercy in Whippany, New Jersey. Clifford said that in the anti-Catholic climate of the presidential campaign, "Catholics themselves—and, least of all, the priests—can do nothing." Their protests would lend credence to the notion that a Smith presidency would subordinate the country to the pope. For that reason, Catholics "must be doubly grateful that a teacher and a Jew of your great gifts should lift his voice for them in their hard extremity." Clifford had been moved both by Wise's staunch support for Al Smith and for their common "pleading for the Jew."[50]

In the end, Smith didn't even win his home state, let alone the election at large. Hoover prevailed by one of the biggest landslides in American history to date: 58.2 percent of the popular vote to 40.8 percent. In the Electoral College, Smith won just eight states and 87 votes—Hoover received 444. In New York State, Smith was substantially outpolled by his fellow Democrat, Roosevelt, who won the Empire State's gubernatorial election, albeit narrowly. Of all the issues in play—religion, Prohibition, immigration, city vs. country, race, and the economy—religion appeared to be the most important cause of Smith's defeat. As Lichtman's classic study of the 1928 election concluded, "Differences between Catholics and Protestants best explain the unique shape of electoral politics in the presidential contest. . . . Both nationally and regionally, the division between Catholics and Protestants dominates a statistical description of voter decisions."[51]

In Massena, where the overwhelming majority of voters were white Protestants, Hoover obliterated Smith, winning 63 percent of the vote. The Republican gubernatorial candidate, Albert Ottinger, also prevailed by a large margin, as did all the other Republican candidates on the ballot.[52] It may be that some Catholic and Jewish voters stayed home on election day, intimidated by the local machinations of the Ku Klux Klan. But given the overall Republican coloring of the region, the paucity of Democratic voices, and the large number of ineligible noncitizens who worked at Alcoa, the results in this corner of the country were never in doubt.

As for Stephen Wise, Roosevelt's victory in the statewide election gave him a measure of consolation for his friend Smith's trouncing in the presidential contest. The rabbi saw this outcome as "a thrust by the older Protestant folk of America against us inferior newcomers—Catholics and Jews, Irish, Italians, Russians and all the rest."[53] Roosevelt likely appreciated the way

Wise had handled the Massena affair, and it's not impossible that the rabbi's success in soothing Christian-Jewish tensions in its aftermath had made the difference in FDR's narrow win. The future president beat his Republican rival Ottinger by just 26,000 votes out of 4.2 million cast.

In the electoral campaign, as in the Massena affair, Wise prided himself on his ecumenical support, which is likely the reason he had chosen George Gordon Battle, a non-Jewish Wall Street lawyer, to help him negotiate a resolution to the lingering animosities generated by the blood libel. In its aftermath, Battle praised Wise for "the fiery zeal which you showed to protect the good name of the Jewish people and the Jewish church [sic]." Battle also appreciated "the charity and kindness which you manifested towards those unfortunate men who, through ignorance and weakness, rather than through malice, perpetrated the . . . absurd and atrocious accusation."[54] Here, Battle put his finger on the essential difference of strategy—or perhaps ideology—between Wise and Marshall. The former sought to soothe the religious tensions created by the Massena incident and contain their potential electoral fallout by allowing Hawes and McCann to attribute their anti-Jewish accusations to "ignorance and weakness" rather than antisemitic malice. Marshall wanted them to confess to much darker motives. We'll never know precisely what moved Hawes and McCann to take the blood accusation seriously; what's important is that after Barbara Griffiths turned up safe and sound, a near unanimity of public voices told them they had been wrong.

Epilogue

THE BLOOD LIBEL IN
RECENT TIMES

T he Massena blood libel was, among other things, a classic
media event. It exploded in the *New York Times* and other
big-city newspapers on October 3, 1928, and remained
on the front pages for several days. Once the Associated Press
picked up the story on October 4, local papers everywhere ran
it, often prominently, and the bizarre libel against a small-town
Jewish community became national news. For a few days, the
Massena story competed successfully with reports about the
momentous presidential election of that fall. But after slightly
more than a week of steady publicity, it abruptly disappeared,
as is generally the case with media events. By mid-October,
Hoover-Smith had displaced Massena for good.

The national discussion sparked by the Massena case revealed
essentially no public support for the notion, still accepted in
interwar Europe, that Jews ritually murdered Christian chil-

dren. And most of those who commented on the Massena case professed to being shocked by the emergence of this "medieval myth" and expressed sympathy for the Jews targeted in the case. The anti-Jewish actions of Mayor Hawes and State Trooper McCann became a national scandal, and both found themselves roundly condemned in published articles and private correspondence. Hawes managed to retain his office, but McCann was disciplined by the state police.

The outcome of this scandal was thus almost entirely favorable to Jews, and likely shored up their standing at the end of a difficult decade. During the first half of the 1920s, American Jews had faced sustained, racially tinged attacks from a revived Ku Klux Klan and, more significantly, from Henry Ford, one of the best-known and most-respected figures in the United States. But the election of 1928 proved to be the Klan's last gasp—until a much smaller, more violent version of the KKK emerged during the civil rights movement—and Ford issued what appeared to be a heartfelt apology for having denigrated the Jews. After the Massena affair of 1928, the ritual murder accusation would never reappear in the United States.

The same was far from true elsewhere in the world. In the 1930s, Montreal's two antisemitic newspapers regularly accused Jews of committing ritual murder, and in Europe, the decade before the Second World War saw a number of blood libels against the Jews. The most notorious example was a May 1934 issue of the Nazi newspaper *Der Stürmer*, whose cover depicted two Jews as the Nazis typically portrayed them—long sloped nose, huge lips, scraggly beard, high forehead with receding hair,

Der Stürmer

and yarmulke stuck to the back of their heads. One was shown piercing a Christian child with a knife and the other collecting the spurting blood in a large silver vessel. The headline reads, "Jewish Murder Plan against Gentile Humanity Revealed."[1]

The real murders were, of course, committed by the Nazis. In May 1943, Heinrich Himmler armed his *Einsatzgruppen* (Mobile Killing Units) with a book depicting Jewish ritual murder before sending them east to slaughter Jews.[2] Despite the Nazi intention to eliminate all of Europe's Jews, especially those in the East, a small number of Polish Jews managed to survive. When they began to straggle home in late 1944, they didn't receive a warm welcome. The Jewish survivors wanted to reclaim their houses and apartments, but their former neighbors threatened to kill them if they persisted. Christian Poles occupied those homes and didn't want to give them back. The Jews' tormentors were motivated not only by greed but also by shame over their complicity with the wartime genocide and fear that the returning Jews would seek vengeance against them. In more than a few cases, threats turned into violence and death. Approximately 1,500 Polish Jews, having survived the Holocaust, were murdered after the war by their fellow Poles.[3]

As if to justify the violence against returning Polish Jews, a series of ritual murder accusations began to circulate widely.[4] The first surfaced in Chelm in the spring of 1945, when a group of Polish militiamen accused several Jews of "draining the blood of a Christian boy." The soldiers tortured one of the Jews until he confessed. In this case, the anti-Jewish violence was minimal, but events escalated from there. A few weeks later, Jews in Rzeszow were accused of kidnapping and mutilating a young Polish girl after militiamen found her body in the basement of a building occupied by Jewish Holocaust survivors. One of the Jews served as a kosher butcher, and the soldiers pointed to his knife as evidence that the Jews had drained her body of blood and used it for religious purposes. Officials placed the town's entire Jewish population under arrest, and as they were being hauled to the police station, a hostile crowd attacked them with clubs and stones. Several Jews were badly injured.

A few days later, a new ritual murder accusation in the neighboring town of Przemysl led to demands that all Jews clear out before the middle of August 1945. Many hastened to leave but found themselves under assault on their way out of town. Rioting aimed at Jews followed in Opatow, Sanok, Lublin, Grojec, Gneiwoszow, Raciaz, and several other towns, where new blood libels and other antisemitic propaganda proliferated.

Jews fled to Poland's larger cities, where they thought there would be safety in numbers, but blood libels followed them wherever they went. In Krakow, police arrested a Jewish woman for supposedly trying to kidnap and murder a Christian child. This allegation led to many more: one resident claimed to have discovered 13 bodies of murdered Christian children, a number that was quickly inflated to 80. After a thirteen-year-old boy darted out of a synagogue yelling, "Help. They want to murder me!" a crowd of sixty Poles broke into the sanctuary looking for Christian corpses. Finding none, they destroyed everything in sight and ultimately set the building ablaze. One Auschwitz survivor was killed, and four other Jews reportedly lost their lives. Several more suffered serious injuries, and on arriving at the hospital, patients and soldiers beat them again, calling the victims "Jewish scum."

What happened in Krakow constituted a small-scale pogrom; anti-Jewish violence in Kielce nearly a year later turned into a full-blown attack. Before the war, some 24,000 Jews—one-third of the town's population—lived in Kielce, a small city in southeastern Poland. Of the 24,000, all but 200 perished at Treblinka, and these rare survivors trickled back to Kielce in the summer of 1946. They took up residence close together on the same street, where they established some fledgling Jewish institutions. But no sooner did the Jews settle in than rumors of ritual murder began to fly. Townspeople posted leaflets about missing children on walls and telephone poles, and priests announced during Sunday mass the names of children who had supposedly disappeared into the deadly clutches of the Jews.

Most of these "missing" children had gone off on their own or with friends, without telling their parents. In one case, a nine-year-old boy named Henryk Blaszczyk hitchhiked to a village where his family had formerly lived and stayed there for two days visiting old friends. When he returned to Kielce, he blunted his parents' anger by inventing a story about being kidnapped by a strange man and locked in a cellar. Henryk said he had been in Kielce all along, confined in a dank basement until someone heard his cries and released him. Hearing this story, a friend of his parents asked if his captor was a Jew. The boy said yes.

Henryk's father decided to report the "abduction" to the police, and on the way to the station, they passed a house in which several Jews had taken up residence. The boy told the police that he had been held there and pointed to a young Jewish man as his captor. Authorities arrested the man, Kalman Singer, and searched the residence for other captives or bodies. When it became clear that the house had no cellar, Henryk changed his story: he had actually been confined in a doghouse above ground.

No matter: a huge crowd congregated outside the "Jewish house," threatening the people inside. Before long, a platoon of soldiers entered the scene, raising tensions to the boiling point as they joined the search for corpses of children. One of the soldiers claimed to have glimpsed four dead bodies in quicklime, and another believed for a time that his own child lay among them. At this point, the crowd of townspeople, having swelled dramatically to about 15,000, pushed into the house and began attacking Jews. Soldiers and policemen did nothing to stop them, and some participated in the assaults. One of the policemen testified later that "the military led Jews out of apartments, and people began hitting them with everything they could."[5]

Meanwhile, Henryk's uncle, who worked at the local steel mill, recruited 600 of his colleagues to join the anti-Jewish attacks. The workers arrived armed with bats, crowbars, and stones; their intervention upped the Jewish toll and quickly engulfed the town as a whole. Anyone who looked "Semitic" was vulnerable. When a group of Jews took refuge in a train station, marauders bludgeoned them with railroad ties and pieces of metal track. Seven Jews lost their lives. Other Jews were loaded into a truck and beaten to death on the outskirts of town.

In testimony given after these events, one Kielce resident said, "The sight of the large, modern apartment house on Planty Street [where several Jews resided] was the ultimate in ruthless havoc. . . . The immense courtyard was littered with blood-stained iron pipes, stones and clubs, which had been used to crush the skulls of Jewish men and women. Blackening puddles of blood still remained. . . . Blood-drenched papers were scattered on the ground—sticky with gore, they clung to the earth though a strong wind blew through the yard."[6]

In the end, forty-two Jewish Holocaust survivors lay dead, along with two non-Jewish Poles. Another forty Jews suffered serious wounds. In many ways, the number of casualties, high as it was, understated the degree of brutality exhibited in the Kielce pogrom. Eyewitness reports testify to the random shooting of "Semitic" people, to men and women stoned to death, to policemen throwing young girls out of third-story windows. The girls who survived the fall were beaten to death by the crowd below.[7]

It is never easy to explain how such cold, murderous cruelty can be possible, but this terrible postwar pogrom reveals, among other things, the deep emotional resonance of the centuries-old myth that Jews murder Christian children for their blood. But why did the blood libel surface to such horrifying effect in postwar Poland? The historian Jan T. Gross gives perhaps the most plausible explanation: "Wherever Jews had been plundered, denounced, betrayed, or killed by their neighbors, their reappearance after the war evoked this dual sense of shame and contempt. . . . And as long as Polish society was unable to mourn its Jewish neighbors' deaths, it had either to purge them or to live in infamy."[8]

The explanation is plausible, but can we really understand the degree of barbarism involved? Perhaps the war had made grotesque violence so much a part of everyday life that even a year after the conflict ended, its horrific norms remained in place. In any case, the result of this postwar series of blood libels was to empty Poland of the 200,000 Jewish survivors who had taken refuge there beginning in 1944. The Nazis hadn't quite exterminated prewar Poland's three-million-strong Jewish population; ordinary Poles finished the job. The so-called silver lining was that with essentially no Jews left in Poland after 1946, the blood libel disappeared in that country.

Beyond Poland, the other major center of Jewish life in prewar Europe was, of course, the Soviet Union. Although the Communist government officially condemned antisemitism as a heinous characteristic of the old tsarist regime, ritual murder accusations nonetheless appeared regularly in the 1920s, 1930s, and beyond. In the early years of the USSR, anti-Jewish accusations surfaced in Byelorussia, Dagestan, and Ukraine in 1926, Uzbekistan in 1928, Ukraine again in 1929, and a second time in Byelorussia in 1937. Although local officials generally credited the accusations as true, in the 1920s regional authorities, especially in places with large Jewish populations and prominent Jewish Communist Party members, either refused to endorse the accusations or punished those who had leveled and reinforced them. Still, in Dagestan and Uzbekistan, the accusations sparked violence against Jews. After Stalin consolidated his power in the 1930s, the regime became less sympathetic to Jews, who were now discouraged from reporting blood libels. Official Stalinist doctrine held that antisemitism was a form of "bourgeois nationalism" that occurred only in fascist countries.[9]

During the Second World War, lack of sympathy toward Jews turned into outright antisemitism, as the Stalinist regime began to rank Jews among the greatest internal enemies of the fatherland. Jews now rightly feared that in cases of blood libel, they, and not their accusers, would be punished; they mostly kept blood libels to themselves. Their reluctance to report accusations to the authorities makes it difficult for historians to know how many blood libels surfaced in the Soviet Union in the late 1940s and 1950s. Anecdotal evidence suggests that they weren't uncommon.[10]

There is also evidence that, beginning in the Second World War, the ritual murder accusation became secularized: Jews were now said to kill Christians for nonreligious reasons. Under wartime conditions of scarcity and famine, authorities accused Jews of a nonritualistic cannibalism, of using the minced bodies of children to make a grotesque soup. Immediately after the war, such a secular version of the ritual murder accusation became common, especially in parts of Ukraine and Soviet Poland where Holocaust survivors returned to reclaim their property. The "secular" blood libel proved a way to stir up animosity against returning Jews and attempt to keep the homes stolen from them.

In 1953, when Stalin announced a phony Jewish "Doctors' plot" against the Soviet people, officials and ordinary citizens once again denounced Jews for murdering children, only now the Jews did so not to harvest their blood but simply because they were diabolical. In early 1953, a Lithuanian Communist Party official named Petrov claimed that instead of curing children, pediatricians "killed them by infecting them with cancer."[11] The notion quickly caught on. When a Jewish pediatrician told a child's parents that she should be hospitalized for pneumonia, the mother replied, "I'd rather let her die at home than in your hospital from poison." After another parent accused the same pediatrician of infecting Russian babies with cancer, the doctor was fired from her job. In yet another Lithuanian case, a parent declared, "Instead of giving children a vaccine against tuberculosis, [the doctor] poisoned them with tuberculosis." Meanwhile, Jewish pharmacists found themselves accused of spiking children's medicines with deadly biological agents.[12] In these instances, the secularized version of the blood libel referred all at once to modern medicine and to medieval images of Jews as people who poisoned wells and deliberately spread the bubonic plague.

With Stalin's death in March 1953, the "Doctors' plot" subsided, only to have the traditional blood libel return. Several cases were reported in the Central Asian republics in the early 1960s, and anti-Jewish protests ensued. In 1963, when a girl's body washed up in Vilnius, a large, angry crowd threatened to unleash a pogrom. Each time, public officials either endorsed the accusations or failed to challenge them.[13]

The fall of the Soviet Union in 1991 didn't mark the end of ritual murder as a popular belief. In 2005, twenty nationalist and communist members of the Russian Duma (parliament) signed an open letter urging that Russia's Jewish organizations be banned on the grounds that Jews were "anti-Christian and inhumane, and their practices extend even to ritual murders." The subheadings of the letter referred to "Jewish Fascism" and called Judaism "a Form of Satanism." The signatories blamed Jews for the fall of the Soviet Union and for wrecking the Russian economy. They also accused Jews of murdering a Russian Orthodox priest in 1990 and of cynically staging attacks against Jews and Jewish organizations to evoke sympathy for themselves. The Duma voted to condemn this letter, but nearly a third of its members refused to support the resolution.[14]

In the same year as the open letter, the Russian ethnographer Aleksandr L'vov, working in Ukraine, found residues of the blood libel still very much alive among ordinary middle-class people. One informant told L'vov that in Soviet times, Jews secretly baked matzo and offered some to their non-Jewish neighbors. "Of course we did not eat it," the informant said.

"There is [some reason for this] written in the Bible, but I forgot." Another of L'vov's informants had forgotten nothing: The Jews "always added a little drop of human blood. As if it was the blood of Jesus Christ."[15]

Recently, the ritual murder accusation was voiced at the highest levels of the Russian Orthodox Church. In November 2017, several members of the Church commission looking into the 1918 killing of Tsar Nicholas II and his family called the assassinations a Jewish ritual murder. The Bolshevik commander said to have done the deed was Jewish, and for some Russian churchmen, this was proof enough that the royal killings were as much religious crimes as political ones.[16]

If the blood libel remains alive in Russia, it has shriveled to almost nothing in Western Europe. In 1965, Vatican II condemned all forms of anti-Jewish persecution and took an unequivocal stand against the idea of Jewish ritual murder. In particular, the assembled Catholic leaders forbade all references to the sanctity of Simon of Trent, the child martyr supposedly murdered by the Jews in 1475. Simon's remains, long an object of Catholic veneration, were uprooted from their privileged perch in Italy and sent to an unpublicized location, probably in Bolivia.[17]

In the years following Vatican II, Catholic traditionalists challenged several of the decisions taken there. The Italian priest Francesco Ricossa demanded that the cult surrounding Saint Simon of Trent be revived, and in 2006 a prominent member of Italy's far-right National Alliance called for an autopsy of Simon's remains. These efforts proved marginal at best: most practicing Catholics seemed happy to forget about "Little Simon," and the chapel formerly consecrated to him now hosts an ecumenical center for interreligious understanding.[18]

Despite these positive developments, references to ritual murder in Western Europe haven't entirely disappeared. In 2003, Israeli officials and Jewish leaders in the United Kingdom denounced the cartoonist Dave Brown for alluding to the blood accusation in a caricature drawn for the *Independent* newspaper. The cartoon showed a naked Ariel Sharon, the former Israeli prime minister, eating a Palestinian baby. Brown's critics maintained that the image referred to the legend that Jews killed children, although in this case, the child was Muslim rather than Christian. Brown responded that the Sharon cartoon was meant to criticize Israeli treatment of Palestinians and had been inspired by Francisco Goya's painting *Saturn Devouring His Son* and not by the anti-Jewish blood libel.[19] Goya's painting depicts the Greek myth of the Titan Cronus, often known as Saturn, eating his child to prevent the baby from replacing him one day. Brown's explanation apparently convinced Britain's media watchdog agency, the Press Complaints Commission, which ruled that his cartoon did not show "antagonism to Sharon's race or religion."

Perhaps the most bizarre recent reference in Western Europe to Jewish ritual murder surfaced in Italy in 2007 with the publication of *Passovers of Blood: The Jews of Europe and Ritual Murder* by the Italian-Israeli historian Ariel Toaff.[20] In this work, Toaff argued that the 1475 ritual murder accusation against the Jews of Trent was most likely true. The historian also maintained that certain Ashkenazi Jews regularly used the blood of Christian children in their Passover rituals—despite the Talmudic ban on all consumption of blood. Toaff portrayed the Jews of medieval northern Italy as "insolent brawlers, who spent most of their time muttering their incomprehensible prayers in noisy, vulgar songs." This Jewish community, he added, was "closed into itself, fearful and aggressive toward the outside world . . . and steeped in its own ideological contradictions." It responded to persecution by "taking refuge in ancient religious rites and myths . . . expressed in a harsh, alienating, and rigorous religious language."[21]

Toaff's unforgiving portrait of fifteenth-century Italian Jewry emerged from a branch of modern Jewish historiography that seeks to depict Jews not as the pure victims of religious hatred but as a people like any other, a people both kind and cruel, quiescent and vengeful, moderate and extreme, a people whose religious beliefs and practices inevitably contributed to Christian attitudes toward them.[22] One key proponent of this newer approach was the medievalist Israel Yuval, who maintained that, in the Middle Ages, Jews and Christians didn't exist in isolation from one another, but rather interacted regularly in the villages and small towns in which most people lived. These interactions produced forms of reciprocity between the two peoples and their respective religions. This reciprocity meant that the blood libel, among other forms of Jew-hatred, bore some relation, even if a distorted one, to what Jews said and did.[23]

Yuval first made this case in a 1993 issue of the Israeli journal *Zion*, sparking a howl of controversy and a polemical battle that continued for more than two years.[24] Several of Yuval's critics accused him of blaming the Jewish victims and of creating a false moral equivalence between the messianic hopes of Jews and the actual deeds of Christians. The Jews sought God's vengeance against Christians at the "end of days," while Christians killed Jews in the here and now in retaliation for their fictive ritual murders of Christian children.[25] Yuval was guilty of neither

ther offense, but in one of the best critiques published in *Zion*,
Jeremy Cohen, a historian of medieval Jewish life, challenged
Yuval's reading of the evidence of Jewish martyrdom, maintaining that the texts Yuval cited were based not on the historical acts
of martyrs, but rather on the ex post facto writings of martyrolo-
gists. The latter were individuals who had converted to Christianity to survive the Crusades and sought to justify their choice.
The historian Ezra Fleischer, for his part, denied the reality of
the Jewish messianism that served as a pillar of Yuval's case and
claimed that Yuval's piece played into the hands of antisemites.

Not all of the commentary was hostile. The medievalist Mary Minty supported Yuval's claim that Christians were
aware of Jewish martyrdom in response to the First Crusade
and especially the Jews' killing of their own children, which
the Christians saw as diabolical. In a long response to his critics,
Yuval more than held his own, arguing among other things that
historical scholarship mustn't be constrained by political and
ideological concerns. In the process, he convinced a fair number of historians that, at the very least, there was reciprocity in
the Middle Ages between Christian and Jewish communities
and that in studying antisemitism, ritual murder, and countless
other phenomena, their interactions must be part of the story.

Unlike Toaff, Yuval never said that ritual murders actually
took place. Although Yuval maintained that Jewish actions may
have contributed to the origins of the blood libel, it remained
for him a pernicious fiction. He and other practitioners of the
modern Jewish historiography either marked their distance
from Toaff or joined a chorus of criticism of his book.[26]

But it wasn't just historians who weighed in. The book's publication by an established Italian house guaranteed that it would

be reviewed prominently and, given the explosive subject matter, that it would unleash the kind of media scandal that sells newspapers and books. *Passovers of Blood* sold out in two days, and at first the publisher couldn't turn out copies fast enough. Headlines in the Italian press screamed: "A Book Sensation: Human sacrifices, the Jews divided." Another asked: "Should Simon of Trent Be Revisited?" Toaff, labeled "the Jewish Vampire," became ubiquitous on television.[27]

Although certain media figures found the book plausible, or at least wanted to, historians, and not just Italian ones, pointed to the book's all-too-obvious flaws. Toaff took at face value Jewish confessions of ritual murder exacted under torture. He assumed that because the various ritual murder stories resembled one another, they must be true; in reality, judges and politicians proffered a false preexisting narrative and repeated it again and again. Toaff used a variety of sources uncritically, especially some questionable Church documents and the writings of converted Jews hostile to their former religion. Toaff didn't just misinterpret his sources; he manipulated them in ways that violated the established standards of history writing and did so in sensationalist prose intended to captivate readers who didn't know better.

Toaff responded to the tidal wave of criticism by doubling down. He called himself the first historian courageous enough to overcome the deep-seated taboo against taking ritual murder seriously. If he continued to be vilified for this courageous stand, so be it. But as critics progressively exposed the weakness of his book, he began to walk back his argument. He now claimed that he didn't really mean to say that ritual murder actually happened, but rather that historians should study it without any prior assumptions. His book was meant as an "ironic academic provocation." With these remarks, Toaff publicly denied the central idea of his book, namely that Jews did, at times, murder Christian children for their blood. It was only a matter of time before he asked his publisher to withdraw *Passovers of Blood* from circulation. He resolved to donate his royalties to the Anti-Defamation League, which had sharply condemned the book.

Toaff's mea culpa didn't prevent the Italian far right from exploiting his work. Father Ricossa, who a few years earlier had sought in vain to reopen the case of Simon of Trent, now declared himself vindicated and Simon's martyrdom real. The extremist Northern League agreed: Simon's remains should be returned to Italy and his veneration as a saint confirmed. Perhaps the most troubling response to Toaff's book was the claim that it demonstrated the utility of torture.

Although Toaff eventually surrendered to the torrent of criticism, why, in the first place, did he make such unsustainable claims? Several critics have speculated that although the book was written in Italian and published in Italy, its intellectual origins lay in the rollicking, free-for-all debate over history that, since the 1980s, has buffeted Israeli academic and public life. Almost everything has been up for grabs, and especially the founding Zionist narrative that portrays Jews and Israel as victims and Arabs as aggressors. The historian Benny Morris, for example, argued that Arabs didn't leave Palestine of their own accord in 1947 and 1948; they were ejected, often ruthlessly, by Zionist forces.[28]

Israelis are accustomed to thoroughgoing historical revisionism, and, given the intense conflicts within Israeli society between left and right, secular and religious, and between Israelis and Palestinians, history writing is much more closely tied to contemporary politics than it is in Europe or the United States. In Toaff's case, commentators have suggested that as a left-wing, secular Jew, he was upset over the explosive growth of an ultra-Orthodox population in Israel whose behavior and attitudes seemed almost medieval. Perhaps their "religious fanaticism" had moved Toaff to see the Jews of 1475 as fanatics, even bloodthirsty fanatics, as well?[29] In Israel, critics, even hostile ones, would have understood the extent to which Toaff's book had been shaped by the contemporary battle between secular and ultra-religious Jews; in the Italian context, it could be seen only as a bizarre apologia for a vile legend discredited long ago.

The brouhaha in Italy over Toaff's book eventually quieted down, but in parts of the Middle East, his work appeared to confirm what had become an article of faith: Jews routinely killed babies, Christian and Muslim. In October 2000, the pro-government Egyptian paper *Al-Ahram* ran a full-page article entitled "Jewish Matzah Made from Arab Blood."[30] In June 2015, Sheikh Kaled Al-Mughrabi, who preaches at the al-Aksa Mosque in Jerusalem, declared in his homily, "The Children of Israel . . . would look for a small child, kidnap and steal him, bring a barrel called the barrel of nails. . . . They would put the small child in the barrel and his body would be pierced by these nails. In the bottom of the barrel, they would put a faucet and pour the blood."[31] A few months later, Salah Al-Bardawil, a Hamas leader in Gaza, said on television that the Jews have an "ancient biblical belief, which instructed them to kill children and collect their blood, in order to knead it into the bread that is eaten on Passover." Al-Bardawil tied this myth to killings of

Palestinians by Israeli civilians and armed forces: "This is the killing of a Palestinian child in order to collect his blood and to knead it into the bread they eat."[32] Similar material appeared on Alef, the prominent Iranian website. "Who Are Human History's Most Bloodthirsty People?" one posted article asked. The answer was obvious, and the article, one of many similar pieces published on the website and elsewhere in Iran, rehearsed the classic ritual murder myth.[33] There are endless examples such as these, making it clear that if the blood libel has virtually disappeared in the West, save perhaps for Russia, it is alive and well in the Palestinian territories, Iran, and elsewhere in the Arab world.

In the United States, the blood libel gripped an entire community just a single time, and after Massena, it would never recur. But for Massena's Jews, the blood libel, however favorable the outcome, left deep scars and gave the episode a long afterlife. My Massena relatives regularly repeated the story to me as a child and young adult, although the emotions embedded in it faded over time. No one in my family tried to revive the incident publicly, as Rabbi Brennglass's daughter-in-law did in the early 1950s, and relations between Massena's Jews and Gentiles, shopkeepers and Alcoa workers, remained perfectly civil, at least on the surface.

Memories of 1928 briefly roiled the town fifty years later when the historian Saul S. Friedman published his book on the Massena blood libel, the only other book-length treatment to date. But Massenans found Friedman's volume so error-ridden and unreliable that it quickly disappeared. Friedman's sensationalist subtitle, "Anti-Semitic Hysteria in a Typical American Town," never rang true, nor did his purple prose: "It was as if a cesspool of hate had suddenly been tapped [by Barbara's disappearance], and now Neanderthal, carnivore, budding rapist, blood avenger, howler at the moon, *haidamak* [Cossacks], crusader[,] all materialized in Massena." The actions of Massena's authorities, Friedman wrote, "struck like hammer blows at the walls of civilization."[34]

But Friedman's conclusion was hyperbolic at best: the Massena blood libel ultimately showed that American civilization, at least in relation to its Jewish population, was stronger than many people thought. Beyond Massena, the ritual murder accusation evoked essentially no public support, not even from the KKK, suggesting that prejudice against Jews in this country was just that: we may not want you to join our clubs or take too many places in our universities, but we don't believe, as many Europeans still did, that your religion requires you to murder innocents and consume their blood.

It's true that in October 1928, some of Massena's Gentiles, angry over the negative publicity their town had received, called for a boycott of Jewish shops. The Gentiles, many of whom considered the response to Barbara Griffiths's disappearance a simple "misunderstanding," wanted to punish Massena's Jewish leaders for having alerted Marshall, Wise, and Governor Smith. But there's no evidence that a boycott ever took hold.[35] In any case, tensions quickly quieted down, and save for the occasional "Christ-killer" accusation, Massena's Jewish community was left in peace.

As for the town itself, never especially prosperous before the Second World War, it began to thrive in the 1950s. Both Reynolds Aluminum and General Motors opened factories there in 1957, providing thousands of new jobs. Part of what attracted these new companies was the St. Lawrence Seaway Project, a system of locks, gates, dredged channels, and newly built canals. The locks serve as up and down elevators for ships, allowing them to navigate the nearly impassible St. Lawrence River, which drops 226 feet from Lake Ontario to Montreal. When finished in 1959, the Seaway connected Duluth, Minnesota, to the Atlantic Ocean. Although the Seaway proved a boon for local industry, now able to import raw materials and transport finished products over 2,350 miles of linked waterways, the project itself provided only a handful of permanent jobs.[36]

Still, in the 1950s and 1960s, the heyday of American industrial prowess, Massena's high school grads could cross the street from their school to the GM employment office and be hired on the spot.[37] About a quarter of Massena High's graduating class each year found well-paying industrial jobs in their hometown.

These opportunities were not destined to last.

When the United States's traditional industries—steel, aluminum, automobiles, and the like—began to suffer from foreign competition in the 1970s, Massena's manufacturing concerns suffered as well. The town's geographical isolation and rigorous climate prevented it from replacing smokestack industries with high-tech or other forms of white-collar manufacturing, as, for example, Pittsburgh would do. Between the 1980s and the early 2000s, Massena spiraled downward, losing jobs, commerce, and population, as globalization and neoliberal policies in Washington exacerbated the deindustrialization of America.[38]

In 1999, Alcoa took over Reynolds, throwing hordes of people out of work. Today, only a few hundred aluminum jobs are left, and Alcoa survives only because the state of New York agreed to subsidize it, between 2011 and 2019, to the tune of $210 million.[39] GM followed a similar, depressing path. In the late 1980s, the automaker drastically cut production at its Massena plant, and shut down completely twenty years later. The town's official, understated, unemployment jumped to 9.8 percent in 1991 and 13.4 percent in 1998. In the 2000s, joblessness remained persistently higher than the national average and soared to nearly 11 percent after the Great Recession of 2008. It came down only in 2014 and remains one of the highest in New York State, dipping to 5.6 percent in August 2018, when the overall New York State rate stood at 4.1 percent.[40] What keeps Massena afloat is its numerous health care facilities and sizable public sector.

In mid-2018, a bitcoin mining operation opened in Massena, packing thousands of tiny servers into an abandoned Alcoa building. Like the aluminum company more than a century earlier, the bitcoin miners, who require massive amounts of electricity, chose Massena to take advantage of the cheap power generated there. The bitcoin concern has created only a handful of jobs and threatens to raise electricity rates for the entire region. It has done nothing to reverse Massena's decline.[41]

Massena's economic woes have sunk into the landscape of the town, which would be familiar to readers of Richard Russo—the novelist who sets several of his stories in an upstate New York stripped of industry and too many of its jobs.[42] Driving through the center of Massena, I saw one vacant storefront after another and empty lots where there once stood houses and stores, including my relatives' Kauffman's Department Store. Most commerce has migrated to the periphery of town and features fast-food restaurants, chain stores, and big-box emporiums.

Kauffman's closed in 1979 and succumbed to the wrecking ball seven years later.[43] After Kauffman's, the other Jewish shops shuttered one by one, shrinking the already-small Jewish community. Today, only 10 Jews live in Massena, and the synagogue no longer exists, having closed its doors in 2012.[44] A few of Massena's current Jewish residents had moved away from the town decades earlier but returned as retirees after cashing in their homes in Boston or New York City. Given Massena's depressed home values—the September 2018 median was $69,900—baby boomers who had left Massena for college and jobs could afford to buy real estate in both Massena and Florida.[45]

These retirees have returned because so many others have left. St. Lawrence County, of which Massena is the second-largest town, has one of the highest poverty rates in New York State, and the lack of manufacturing jobs has forced many Massena residents to flee.[46] Those who remain, almost all of them white, tend to live with sharp financial constraints. In 2016, St. Lawrence County, along with the rest of upstate New York, voted heavily for Donald Trump, 52.5 percent to Hillary Clinton's 41 percent (overall, New York State awarded Clinton almost 59 percent of the vote).[47] St. Lawrence County's Trump vote would have been even higher had it not been for its two college towns—Canton (St. Lawrence University) and Potsdam (State University of New York). With virtually no unionized workers left in town, Massena has returned to its Republican roots.

The town's Jewish history has been preserved in a small cemetery whose headstones bear witness to the twenty or so Jewish families whose members lived quietly there from the early twentieth century to the early twenty-first. The cemetery betrays not a single hint of the blood libel of 1928, nor is there any monument or plaque that commemorates it in town. The local paper, the *Massena Observer*, never mentioned it, and historians have to dig deep in Massena's small historical museum and municipal archives to find any reference to what, for a time, had been a huge national story.

The memories that remain in the second decade of the twenty-first century reside in the minds of Jews who grew up in Massena and remember hearing about the blood libel as children. In 2012, Shirley Vernick turned those memories into a novel written for young adults, and periodically people interested in the case make a visit, as I did, to Barbara Griffiths Klemens, who lives close by in Hermon, New York.[48] Though still going strong at age ninety-four, Barbara has no memory of getting lost in the woods and unwittingly sparking a scandal of national import.

Acknowledgments

First, and most important, I'd like to thank the Massena natives and Massena residents whose guidance made it possible for me to write this book. My greatest debt is to my cousin Judith Baker, who grew up in Massena and traveled there with me on my initial research trip. Judith introduced me to longtime Massena resident Charles Romigh, who together with Judith set up interviews for me with longtime Massena residents Doris Robinson, Lenore Levine, and Alice Rosen. A Massena librarian kindly gave me Barbara Griffiths Klemens's contact information, and I especially appreciate the time Barbara gave me, sitting for two long interviews and offering a wealth of information, not to mention her extensive file of newspaper clippings. Thanks, as well, to Barbara's daughter Ann Sloan, who invited me to her mother's home and loaned me a treasure trove of family pictures. Closer to New York City, Alan C. Brennglass spoke with me at length about his grandfather Rabbi Brennglass and other members of his Massena family.

Massena's town historian MaryEllen Casselman graciously allowed me to roam around the Celine Philibert Cultural Center and Museum, over which she presides, and helped me find all kinds of things. JeanMarie Martello, the archives manager of the St. Lawrence County Historical Society in Canton, New York, proved equally accommodating, and I wish to thank her as well. I appreciate the time that John D. Michaud III, Massena's unofficial historian, spent with me, and I'm grateful for his willingness to share several historical photographs from his extensive personal collection. I'm grateful as well to Shirley Vernick, who spoke with me about her own work on the Massena blood libel and to the librarians and archivists at New York's Center for Jewish History.

At New York University, I'd like to thank my colleagues Hasia Diner, who gave me the benefit of her unparalleled knowledge of American Jewish history, and Zvi Ben-Dor Benite, who read the entire manuscript and offered valuable suggestions and advice. I'm grateful as well to NYU's Center for the Humanities, and especially to its director, Gwynneth Malin, for the fellowship that allowed me to finish this book. My gratitude goes also to the Center's faculty director, Gabriela Basterra, and the fifteen other fellows who engaged with my work and gave me excellent comments about it.

My editor at W. W. Norton, John Glusman, read my manuscript expertly, and his comments and queries improved it in crucial ways. I'm lucky to have benefited from his interest in the subject matter and his astute editorial judgment. Thanks also to Norton's Helen Thomaides, who made the myriad tasks of finishing a manuscript relatively easy, and to Nancy Palmquist for her superb copyediting. Francelle Carapetyan is a brilliant photo researcher, and I thank her once again for her contributions to my work.

I'm grateful, as always, to my wonderful literary agent, Sandy Dijkstra, who found the ideal home for this book and who was the first person to read the entire manuscript. The notes she gave me were invaluable.

My wife, Catherine Johnson, an accomplished writer, inspires me every day, and her interest in everything constantly teaches me about things I'd never learn on my own.

My parents, Claire and Norman Berenson, told me about the Massena blood libel when I was very young, and the story has always remained in the back of my mind. My mother preserved the family pictures reproduced in this book, and my father tried to convey what the Massena incident meant to him as an eight-year-old boy. He passed away in March 2018 at age ninety-eight. It was a good, long life but still much too short. I'm proud to dedicate this book to him.

Notes

Prologue: A Child Disappears

1. I have reconstructed the story of Barbara's disappearance from a thick file of newspaper clippings maintained by Barbara Griffiths Klemens, whom I interviewed on June 3, 2015, and October 27, 2018. Ms. Klemens, age ninety-one at the time of our first meeting, has few direct memories of the 1928 incident. The principal press sources are the *Massena Observer*, September 27, 1928; *Watertown Times*, September 26 through October 4; Syracuse *Post-Standard*, September 26–October 4; *New York Times*, September 26–October 4; *Gouverneur Free Press*, September 28, 1928.

2. Shulkin to Rabbi Stephen Wise, September 25, 1928, Stephen Wise Papers, Center for Jewish History, New York, reel no. 74-37, box 49 (hereafter SWP).

3. Hawes to Wise, October 4, 1928, in SWP, reel no. 74-37, box 49.

4. Louis Marshall, president, American Jewish Committee, to Billikopf, October 2, 1928, in Louis Marshall Papers, The Jacob Rader Marcus Center of the American Jewish Archives, Cincinnati, Ohio, series B, box 6, folder 8 (hereafter LMP).

5. Abraham G. Duker, "Twentieth-Century Blood Libels in the United

States," in Alan Dundes, ed., *The Blood Libel Legend: A Casebook in Anti-Semitic Folklore* (Madison: University of Wisconsin Press, 1991).

6. Joan Dobbie, Louis Greenblatt, and Blanche Levine, *Before Us: Studies of Early Jewish Families in St. Lawrence County, 1855–1920* (Ogdensburg, NY: Ryan Press, 1981), 186–88.

7. For the definitive book on Jewish peddlers, see Hasia R. Diner, *Roads Taken: The Great Jewish Migrations to the New World and the Peddlers Who Forged the Way* (New Haven: Yale University Press, 2015).

8. The narrative of Massena's history comes mainly from the following sources: Claire Puccia Parham, *From Great Wilderness to Seaway Towns: A Comparative History of Cornwall, Ontario, and Massena, New York, 1784–2001* (Albany: State University of New York Press, 2004); Eleanor L. Dumas and Nina E. Dumas, *History of Massena, the Orphan Town* (Massena: Massena Printing, 1977); Teresa S. Sharp and David E. Martin, *Images of America: Massena* (Charlestown, SC: Arcadia Publishing, 2005).

9. See David Bell, *Napoleon: A Concise Biography* (New York: Oxford University Press, 2015), 71.

10. See Pierre Birnbaum, *A Tale of Ritual Murder in the Age of Louis XIV: The Trial of Raphaël Lévy, 1669*, trans. Arthur Goldhammer (Stanford, CA: Stanford University Press, 2012).

11. Charles T. Child, "The Electric and Hydraulic Power Plant of the Saint Lawrence Power Company, Massena, N.Y.," *Electrical Review* 37/17 (October 24, 1900).

12. On Alcoa, see George David Smith, *From Monopoly to Competition: The Transformations of Alcoa, 1888–1986* (New York: Cambridge University Press, 1988).

13. Archives of the Massena Aluminum Historical Association, in Archives of the Saint Lawrence County Historical Association, Canton, NY (hereafter MAHA).

14. Dobbie, *Before Us*, 189. *Massena Observer*, July 4, 1935.

15. Census of Population and Housing, www.census.gov, Village of Massena. Thanks to oddities of New York State's political geography, the town of Massena and the village of Massena are slightly different. The town is somewhat larger in area and population than the village, but a small part of the village lies outside the town. In the nineteenth and early twentieth centuries, Massena's largely agricultural character made the town, mostly farmland, considerably larger than the village, mostly residences and stores. After remaining stable at roughly 2,700 from 1840 to 1890, the town's population grew by 40 percent between 1890 and 1900. It grew another 23 percent to nearly 5,000 by 1910 and

soared by nearly 87 percent to almost 9,000 by 1920. It reached 12,000 in 1930. As industry overtook agriculture in the twentieth century, the population difference between the town and the village shrank considerably. In 1930, the town's population was 12,029 and the village's 10,637. In 1960, the town peaked at 17,937, the village at 15,478.

16. Fifteenth Census of the United States: 1930. *Population*, vol. 3 (Washington, D.C.: U.S. Government Printing Office, 1931–33), 297–303.

17. Fifteenth Census of the United States: 1930. *Population*, vol. 3, 276, 290.

18. In the late nineteenth and early twentieth centuries, it was common for Jews with commercial experience or interest to settle in small-town America. See Lee Shai Weissbach, *Jewish Life in Small-Town America: A History* (New Haven: Yale University Press, 2005), 105.

19. Weissbach, *Jewish Life in Small-Town America*, 95.

20. The lone existing book on the Massena blood libel, Saul Friedman's *The Incident at Massena: Anti-Semitic Hysteria in a Typical American Town* (New York: Stein and Day, 1978), is based largely on the memories of Massena Jews, memories collected in interviews conducted in 1971 and 1978. For most of Massena's Gentiles, Friedman's book came as a revelation; they had never heard of the blood libel (my interview with Charles Romigh, Massena, New York, June 1, 2015). But in a review essay prompted by *The Incident at Massena*, Samuel J. (Jackie) Jacobs, long a leader of Massena's Jewish community, sharply criticized the work. Jacobs was a scholarly man, having graduated from Yale Law School and practiced law in New York City before returning to Massena to run the family business (see Dobbie, *Before Us*, 158; interview with Norman Berenson, Media, Pennsylvania, May 15, 2015; interview with Doris Robinson, Massena, New York, June 1, 2015). Jacobs found multiple errors and inaccuracies in Friedman's work and questioned his methods of oral history. Friedman had conducted many of his interviews over the phone, rather than in person, and did not explain why he chose to interview certain individuals but not others or why he left out certain key inhabitants of the town. In addition, Jacobs wrote, Friedman spoke with people too young to have direct memories of the blood libel, quoted an individual who wasn't interviewed, and accepted his interviewees' statements at face value; Jacobs considers many of those statements to have been biased or false. See Samuel J. Jacobs, "The Blood Libel Case at Massena—a Reminiscence and a Review," *Judaism* 28/4 (Fall 1979): 465–74. An even sharper critique of Friedman's book came from Eleanor Dumas, an amateur local historian. Dumas wrote that Friedman listed her mother as a source even though

she had been dead for years before he began his research. Other long-dead people supposedly had supplied photographs to him. Friedman's pages on the history of Massena, she says, are carelessly written and riddled with errors. Most egregiously, Dumas adds, Friedman sensationalized his story, positing an antisemitic "hysteria" when the dominant emotions were apprehension and fear. In his response, Friedman disputed several of these criticisms. See Saul S. Friedman, Laurence Baron, Eleanor Dumas, and Samuel Jacobs, "We Must Tell the World This Story So It Will Never Happen Again: Four Viewpoints of *The Incident at Massena,*" *The Quarterly: Official Publication of the St. Lawrence County Historical Association* XXIV/3 (July 1979): 3–8, 23. I have also found errors in Friedman's book, errors often committed in an effort to make a point for which there is insufficient evidence. For example, Friedman was intent on demonstrating that the idea of ritual murder came from Albert Comnas, a café owner of Greek origins. Referring to Samuel Jacobs's brief account of the ritual murder accusation of 1928 in Dumas, *History of Massena,* Friedman writes, "He [Jacobs] quoted the Greek [Comnas] as saying 'In the Old Country, people would suspect the Jews of foul play.'" In fact, Jacobs doesn't identify Comnas as the source of this quote. See Friedman, *Incident at Massena,* 196n26; Dumas, *History of Massena,* 141. Because questions have been raised about the accuracy and reliability of the Friedman book, I didn't rely on it and, for that reason, rarely refer to it in the pages that follow.

21. Interview with Alice Rosen, Utica, New York, May 31, 2015.
22. Interview with Doris Robinson, Massena, New York, June 1, 2015.
23. See the original "Minutes and Records," dated August 1919 of Congregation Adath Israel in the Celine Philibert Cultural Center and Museum, Massena, New York.
24. Dobbie, *Before Us,* 197–99.
25. Dumas, *History of Massena,* 140–41.

Chapter 1: The Accusation

1. *Watertown Times,* October 5, 1928.
2. M. M. Silver, *Louis Marshall and the Rise of Jewish Ethnicity in America* (Syracuse, NY: Syracuse University Press, 2013), 548.
3. *Massena Observer,* April 15, 1980, and April 23, 1981.
4. MAHA; interview with Barbara Griffiths Klemens and her daughter Ann Sloan, Hermon, New York, October 27, 2018.
5. Photographs from the family collection of Barbara Griffiths Klemens and Ann Sloan.
6. Interview with Barbara Griffiths Klemens, October 27, 2018.

7. *Watertown Times*, September 25, 1928.

8. *Watertown Times*, September 25, 1928.

9. Report on the John B. Andrews House, Archives of the St. Lawrence County Historical Associations, Canton, New York; Fifteenth Census of the United States: 1930. *Population*, vol. 3, Massena Town, sheet no. 1B. On home values, see the *Wall Street Journal*, March 28, 2016.

10. On Hawes, see the *Massena Observer*, March 14, 1929, and November 11, 1948.

11. *Gouverneur Tribune-Press*, June 30, 1965. My Freedom of Information Law request to the New York State Police turned up the response that McCann's personnel records had been destroyed. Letter to me from Keith M. Corlett, first deputy superintendent, New York State Police, March 4, 2019.

12. On Goldberg, see the write-up on him in MAHA.

13. Jacobs, "The Blood Libel Case at Massena," 468.

14. See the discussion on p. 36 of Thomas of Monmouth and the renegade Jew Theobald.

15. Jacobs, "The Blood Libel Case at Massena," 468.

16. *Jewish Daily Bulletin*, October 2, 1928. This conversation is also recorded in J. Shulkin to Stephen Wise, September 25, 1928, SWP.

17. Louis Marshall to Major John A. Warner, superintendent, New York State Police, October 1, 1928, in LMP.

18. Victoria Saker Woeste, *Henry Ford's War on Jews and the Legal Battle Against Hate Speech* (Stanford: Stanford University Press, 2012); Neil Baldwin, *Henry Ford and the Jews: The Mass Production of Hate* (New York: Public Affairs, 2001); Henry Ford, *The International Jew, the World's Foremost Problem* (Dearborn, MI: Dearborn Publishing Company, 1922).

19. The literature on the revived Ku Klux Klan is vast. The best works include Kenneth T. Jackson, *The Ku Klux Klan in the City, 1915–30* (New York: Oxford University Press, 1967); David M. Chalmers, *Hooded Americanism: The History of the Ku Klux Klan* (Durham, NC: Duke University Press, 1967); Thomas R. Pegram, *One Hundred Percent American: The Rebirth and Decline of the Ku Klux Klan in the 1920s* (Chicago: Ivan R. Dee, 2011); Linda Gordon, *The Second Coming of the KKK: The Ku Klux Klan of the 1920s and the American Political Tradition* (New York: W. W. Norton, 2017).

20. Stanley Cappiello, "I remember Massena's KKK," in John D. Michaud III, *Yesterday in Massena: A Bicentennial Celebration 1802–2002* (Massena, NY, 2002), 27.

21. David Fraser, "The Blood Libel in North America: Jews, Law, and Citizenship in the Early 20th Century," *Law & Literature* 28/1 (February 2016): 33–85.

22. Gavin I. Langmuir, "Thomas of Monmouth: Detector of Ritual Murder," in Dundes, *The Blood Libel Legend*, 4–5. Although Jews were accused of practicing ritual murder in chronicles written during the second century BCE and the fifth century CE, Langmuir shows that these cases were unknown in twelfth-century England and therefore that Thomas of Monmouth enjoys the dubious distinction of having invented the ritual murder tale in the Christian West. The Israeli historian Israel Yuval maintains, however, that the Norwich accusation may not have been the first. According to both a Hebrew and a Latin source, writes Yuval, a Jew from Würzburg, Germany, was accused of ritually killing a Christian in the spring of 1147. There is some evidence, Yuval adds, that the accusation against the Jews of Norwich surfaced not in 1144, as Thomas of Monmouth claimed, but in 1147—perhaps slightly after the accusation in Germany. See Israel Jacob Yuval, *Two Nations in Your Womb: Perceptions of Jews and Christians in Late Antiquity and the Middle Ages* (Berkeley: University of California Press, 2006), 166–70. Yuval's book was translated from the original Hebrew edition of 2000. On William of Norwich, see also E. M. Rose, *The Murder of William of Norwich: The Origins of the Blood Libel in Medieval Europe* (New York: Oxford University Press, 2015).

23. Langmuir, "Thomas of Monmouth," in Dundes, ed., *Blood Libel Legend*, 22.

24. Langmuir, "Thomas of Monmouth," in Dundes, ed., *Blood Libel Legend*, 33ff.

25. Langmuir, "Thomas of Monmouth," in Dundes, ed., *Blood Libel Legend*, 34.

26. Langmuir, "Thomas of Monmouth," in Dundes, ed., *Blood Libel Legend*.

27. Gavin Langmuir, "Ritual Cannibalism," in his *Toward a Definition of Anti-Semitism* (Berkeley: University of California Press, 1990), 262–81. My discussion of the Fulda case draws extensively on Langmuir's work.

28. Langmuir, "Ritual Cannibalism," in his *Toward a Definition of Anti-Semitism*, 270ff.

29. Yuval, *Two Nations in Your Womb*, esp. ch. 4. This chapter is a revised, extended version of Yuval's controversial article "Vengeance and Damnation, Blood and Defamation: From Jewish Martyrdom to Blood Libel Accusations," *Zion* LVIII (1993), 33–99, 152. The article was written in Hebrew and prefaced with a long summary in English. (I'm grateful to Zvi Ben-Dor Benite for making me aware of this article.) The controversy it sparked will be discussed in the Epilogue.

30. Yuval, *Two Nations in Your Womb*, 141.

31. Yuval, *Two Nations in Your Womb*, 161, 185.

32. On this point, see Robert Chazan, *European Jewry and the First Crusade*

(Berkeley and Los Angeles: University of California Press, 1987), 213–14. See also Hannah R. Johnson, *The Ritual Murder Accusation at the Limit of Jewish History* (Ann Arbor: University of Michigan Press, 2012), 108. Johnson devotes most of her entire third chapter to an incisive commentary on Yuval.

33. David Nirenberg, *Anti-Judaism: The Western Tradition* (New York: W. W. Norton, 2013), 204–5.

34. Such a symbolic, anthropological form of explanation seems to me preferable to the far more common psychoanalytic one in which Christians are said to *project* their hostility toward Jews onto the Jews themselves, whom the Christians see as wanting to destroy them. The massacre of Jews thus becomes a defensive response. Another form that the psychoanalytic idea of projection takes is to maintain that Christians felt guilty about their own cannibalistic consumption of the body and blood of Christ and, as a psychological defense, projected their guilt onto Jews, who, as a result, become the people who cannibalistically consume the blood of Christ-like Christian children. The anthropological approach is preferable to the psychoanalytic one, because a huge amount of distinguished anthropological work has shown that the analysis of how people use symbols yields a solid understanding of their culture, that is, of their fundamental values, attitudes, and beliefs. The psychoanalytic approach, by contrast, tends to be more conjectural than evidence-based. It applies a theory about the psychology of individuals to large social groups. On symbolism and cultural understanding, see Clifford Geertz, *The Interpretation of Cultures* (New York: Basic Books, 1973); William H. Sewell Jr., *Logics of History: Social Theory and Social Transformation* (Chicago: University of Chicago Press, 2005); Robert Darnton, *The Great Cat Massacre and Other Episodes in French Cultural History* (New York: Vintage Books, 1985); Robert Darnton, "The Symbolic Element in History," *Journal of Modern History* 58 (1986). For an excellent critique of historians' uncritical application of the psychoanalytic concept of projection, see Hannah R. Johnson, "The Stories People Tell: The Blood Libel and the History of Anti-Semitism," *Law & Literature* 28/1 (2016): 11–26. For an example of the kind of analysis Johnson critiques, see Helmut Walser Smith, *The Butcher's Tale: Murder and Anti-Semitism in a German Town* (New York: W. W. Norton, 2002).

35. "Host, Desecration of," *Jewish Encyclopedia*, jewishencyclopedia.com.

36. Smith, *Butcher's Tale*, 98; "Host, Desecration of," *Jewish Encyclopedia*.

37. Nirenberg, *Anti-Judaism*, 189–207.

38. Nirenberg, *Anti-Judaism*, 200.

39. Quoted in Nirenberg, *Anti-Judaism*, 131.

40. Quoted in Nirenberg, *Anti-Judaism*, 133.

41. Nirenberg, *Anti-Judaism*, 113.

42. Nirenberg, *Anti-Judaism*, 115.

43. Nirenberg, *Anti-Judaism*, 198.

44. Nirenberg, *Anti-Judaism*, 209.

45. Tibertino's Latin text, *Passio beati Simonis pueri Tridentini*, 1475, forms the documentary base of one of the best books written on the blood libel, R. Po-Chia Hsia's *Trent 1475: Stories of Ritual Murder* (New Haven: Yale University Press, 1992).

46. Smith, *Butcher's Tale*, 102.

47. Tiberino, quoted in Hillel J. Kieval, "Representation and Knowledge in Medieval and Modern Accounts of Jewish Ritual Murder," *Jewish Social Studies: History, Culture, Society*, new series 1 (1994–95): 58–59.

48. R. Po-Chia Hsia, *The Myth of Ritual Murder: Jews and Magic in Reformation Germany* (New Haven: Yale University Press, 1988), 41.

49. Smith, *Butcher's Tale*, 109.

50. Smith, *Butcher's Tale*, 111.

51. Smith, *Butcher's Tale*, 104–11.

52. Hillel J. Kieval, "Antisémitisme ou savoir social? Sur la genèse du procès modern pour meutre ritual," *Annales HSS*, 49e année, no. 5 (September–October 1994): 1099.

53. Sabina Logiga, "Une vieille affaire: Les 'Pâques de sang' d'Ariel Toaff," *Annales HSS*, 63e année, no. 1 (2008): 147.

54. On antisemitism as a form of "social knowledge," see Kieval, "Antisémitisme," 1098–1105.

55. Alain Corbin, *Village of Cannibals* (Cambridge: Harvard University Press, 1992).

56. On labor unrest, see Alan Trachtenberg, *The Incorporation of America: Culture and Society in the Gilded Age* (New York: Hill and Wang, 2007), esp. 88–91. The Tuskegee Institute (later Tuskegee University) kept what most historians consider reliable, if conservative, annual statistics on lynching from 1892 to 1959. The *Chicago Tribune* also compiled statistics on lynching beginning in 1882. During Reconstruction (1865–77), opponents of black enfranchisement used lynching to terrorize African Americans who dared to take advantage of their newly won rights. See Nell Irvin Painter, "Who Was Lynched?" *Nation* 253/16

(November 11, 1991): 577; Michael J. Pfeifer, *Rough Justice: Lynching and American Society, 1874–1947* (Chicago: University of Illinois Press, 2004); Leon F. Litwack, *Trouble in Mind: Black Southerners in the Age of Jim Crow* (New York: Alfred A. Knopf, 1998).

Chapter 2: Blood Libel in the Modern World

1. Quoted in Smith, *Butcher's Tale*, 112.
2. Smith, *Butcher's Tale*, 112–13.
3. Eugene M. Avrutin, *The Velizh Affair: Blood Libel in a Russian Town* (New York: Oxford University Press, 2018). I discovered this book only in the final stages of preparing my own. The similarities in our subtitles is coincidental.
4. Avrutin, *Velizh Affair*, 153.
5. Smith, *Butcher's Tale*, 113–15.
6. Smith, *Butcher's Tale*, 123; Mary Margaroni, "The Blood Libel on Greek Islands in the Nineteenth Century," in Robert Nemes and Daniel Unowsky, eds., *Sites of European Antisemitism in the Age of Mass Politics, 1880–1918* (Waltham, MA: Brandeis University Press, 2014).
7. Smith, *Butcher's Tale*, for Konitz; for Kiev, Edmund Levin, *A Child of Christian Blood: Murder and Conspiracy in Tsarist Russia: The Beilis Blood Libel* (New York: Schocken Books, 2014).
8. Albert S. Lindemann, *The Jew Accused: Three Anti-Semitic Affairs (Dreyfus, Beilis, Frank) 1894–1915* (New York: Cambridge University Press, 1991), 134.
9. Lindemann, *Jew Accused*, 134–39.
10. Lindemann, *Jew Accused*, 139.
11. The Russian pogroms continued well into the twentieth century and reached their peak of violence during the Russian Revolution. See Steven J. Zipperstein, *Pogrom: Kishinev and the Tilt of History* (New York: Liveright, 2018), 4.
12. Daniel Unowsky, "Local Violence, Regional Politics, and State Crisis: The 1898 Anti-Jewish Riots in Habsburg Galicia," in Nemes and Unowsky, eds., *Sites of European Antisemitism*, 13–35.
13. Unowsky, "Local Violence, Regional Politics, and State Crisis," in Nemes and Unowsky, eds., *Sites of European Antisemitism*, 20.
14. Romania was home to regular ritual murder accusations during the early modern period, and a major blood libel, followed by anti-Jewish rioting, took place in Galaji in 1859.
15. Edith Stern, *The Glorious Victory of Truth: The Tiszaeszlár Blood Libel*

Trial, 1882–1883: A Historical-Legal-Medical Research (Jerusalem: Ruben Mass, 1998); William O. McCagg, *Jewish Nobles and Geniuses in Modern Hungary* (New York: Columbia University Press, 1972); William O. McCagg, *A History of Habsburg Jews, 1670–1918* (Bloomington: Indiana University Press, 1989); Andrew C. Janos, *The Politics of Backwardness in Hungary, 1825–1945* (Princeton: Princeton University Press, 1982).

16. Lindemann, *Jew Accused*, 47–56.
17. Kieval, "Antisémitisme," 1099–1100.
18. Lindemann, *Jew Accused*, 51.
19. Kieval, "Antisémitisme," 1100.
20. Hillel J. Kieval, "Tiszaeszlár Blood Libel," *The YIVO Encyclopedia of Jews in Eastern Europe*, accessed at yivoencyclopedia.org; Andrew Handler, *Blood Libel at Tiszaeszlár* (New York: Columbia University Press, 1980).
21. Hillel J. Kieval, "The Rules of the Game: Forensic Medicine and the Language of Science in the Structuring of Modern Ritual Murder Trials," *Jewish History* 26 (2012): 287–307.
22. Quoted in Kieval, "Antisémitisme," 1095.
23. Quoted in Kieval, "Antisémitisme," 1094.
24. Kieval, "Antisémitisme," 1102.
25. Logiga, "Une vieille affaire," 145.
26. Lindemann, *Jew Accused*, 54; Kieval, "Tiszaeszlár Blood Libel."
27. Smith, *Butcher's Tale*, 132.
28. Smith, *Butcher's Tale*, 129.
29. On the Polná case, see František Červinka, "The Hilsner Affair," in Dundes, ed., *Blood Libel Legend*, 135–61.
30. Kieval, "Representation and Knowledge," 65.
31. For racialized depictions of criminals in the late nineteenth century, see Aaron Freundschuh, *The Courtesan and the Gigolo: The Murders in the Rue Montaigne and the Dark Side of Empire in Nineteenth-Century Paris* (Stanford: Stanford University Press, 2017). For the press and crime, see Dominique Kalifa, *L'Encre et le sang: Récits de crime et société à la Belle époque* (Paris: Fayard, 1995).
32. Smith, *Butcher's Tale*, chapter 2.
33. On the Beilis case, see Levin, *Child of Christian Blood*.
34. Quoted in Charlotte Klein, "Damascus to Kiev: *Civilta Cattolica* on Ritual Murder," in Dundes, ed., *Blood Libel Legend*, 190.
35. "Blood Libel—A History of Groundless Anti-Semitic Fables," see http://jcrelations.tripod.com/blood.html.

36. Quoted in Ulrich Wyrwa, "*L'Osservatoire Cattolico* and Davide Albertario," in Nemes and Unowsky, eds., *Sites of European Antisemitism*, 69.

37. Wyrwa, "*L'Osservatoire Cattolico* and Davide Albertario," in Nemes and Unowsky, eds., *Sites of European Antisemitism*, 72.

38. Wyrwa, "*L'Osservatoire Cattolico* and Davide Albertario," in Nemes and Unowsky, eds., *Sites of European Antisemitism*, 73.

39. On the problem of the Jews' judicial bind, see Hannah R. Johnson, *Blood Libel: The Ritual Murder Accusation at the Limit of Jewish History* (Ann Arbor: University of Michigan Pres, 2012), ch. 1.

40. André Kaspi, "Jules Isaac and His Role in Jewish-Christian Relations," in Eli Lederhender, ed., *Jews, Catholics, and the Burden of History* (New York: Oxford University Press, 2005), 13.

41. Kaspi, "Jules Isaac and His Role in Jewish-Christian Relations," in Lederhender, ed., *Jews, Catholics, and the Burden of History*, 13.

42. Vicki Caron, "Catholics and the Rhetoric of Antisemitic Violence in Fin-de Siècle France," in Nemes and Unowsky, eds., *Sites of European Antisemitism*, 39.

43. This discussion of Drumont follows Caron's in Nemes and Unowsky, eds., *Sites of European Antisemitism*.

44. Quoted in Nemes and Unowsky, eds., *Sites of European Antisemitism*, 46.

45. The historian Elissa Bemporad tells of a seminar about Jewish history and customs she gave to graduate students in Latvia. She passed around pieces of matzo and asked the students to taste them. Most refused, saying they remembered something from their childhoods about the dangers of eating matzo.

46. Quoted in Caron, "Catholics and the Rhetoric," 53.

47. Quoted in Caron, "Catholics and the Rhetoric," 57.

48. Stephen Wilson, *Ideology and Experience: Antisemitism in France at the Time of the Dreyfus Affair* (East Brunswick, NJ: Associated University Presses, 1982), 119. For evidence that the Dreyfus Affair mainly affected cities, where French authorities could keep violence under wraps, see Nancy Fitch, "Mass Culture, Mass Parliamentary Politics, and Modern Anti-Semitism," *American Historical Review* 97/1 (February 1992): 55–95.

Chapter 3: Who Done It: The Immigrants?

1. MAHA.

2. On the history and techniques of aluminum production, see George Smith, *From Monopoly to Competition*, esp. ch. 1.

3. Smith, *From Monopoly to Competition*, 2.

4. Smith, *From Monopoly to Competition*, 8–17.
5. Smith, *From Monopoly to Competition*, 34.
6. Smith, *From Monopoly to Competition*, 15–17.
7. Smith, *From Monopoly to Competition*, 97–101.
8. *Alcoa News* (hereafter *AN*), February 2, 1931.
9. *AN*, July 9, 1934.
10. *Aluminum Bulletin* (hereafter *AB*), June 1, 1919; *AN*, June 10, 1935.
11. *AB*, June 1, 1919; *AN*, August 19, 1935.
12. *AN*, March 16, 1936.
13. *The World Book Encyclopedia* (Chicago: Scott Fetzer Company, 1996), vol. 10, 82.
14. *AB*, June 1, 1919; *AN*, March 8, 1937.
15. *AN*, no date.
16. Bruno Ramirez, *Crossing the Forty-ninth Parallel* (Ithaca: Cornell University Press, 2001).
17. *AN*, October 12, 1941.
18. *AN*, May 1, 1945.
19. *AN*, February 1, 1943.
20. *AN*, no dates.
21. Fifteenth Census of the United States: 1930. *Population*, vol. 3, 320.
22. James N. Gregory, *The Southern Diaspora: How the Great Migrations of Black and White Southerners Transformed America* (Chapel Hill: University of North Carolina Press, 2005).
23. MAHA, "Birth Countries 25 Year Club Members," https://sites.google.com/site/massenaaluminum/history/countries.
24. Bureau of Labor Statistics, CPI Inflation Calculator, https://www.bls.gov/data/inflation_calculator.htm.
25. *AN*, August 17, 1942.
26. Alice Olenin and Thomas F. Corcoran, *Hours and Earnings in the United States, 1932–40* (Bulletin No. 697) (Washington, D.C.: United States Department of Labor, Bureau of Labor Statistics, 1942), 5.
27. Olenin and Corcoran, *Hours and Earnings in the United States, 1932–40*, 10. The closest equivalent to potroom workers in these U.S. government statistics is blast furnace workers.
28. Olenin and Corcoran, *Hours and Earnings in the United States, 1932–40*, 70.
29. For a general study of small-town Jews, see Weissbach, *Jewish Life in Small-Town America*.

30. This account of Massena's Jews follows Dobbie et al., *Before Us*, 143–206.

31. Interview with Judith Kauffman Baker, Boston, Massachusetts, October 1, 2018.

32. *Massena Observer*, July 4, 1935; Ogdensburg *Republican-Journal*, July 2, 1935.

33. "Massena's Oldest Store to Close After 80 Years," *Massena Observer*, December 7, 1978.

34. The tendency of Massena's Jews to return home after college or military service seems to contradict a key finding of Weissbach's study, namely "that a large proportion of those Jews who peopled America's small-town Jewish communities at one time or another did not remain in those settings throughout their lives." Weissbach, *Jewish Life*, 82.

35. Samuel L. Jacobs, "The Blood Libel Case at Massena—a Reminiscence and a Review," *Judaism*, 2001: 445–74; Friedman, *Incident at Massena*.

36. Interview with Alan C. Brennglass, the rabbi's grandson, New Rochelle, New York, June 8, 2015.

37. Interview with Alan C. Brennglass. I've complemented the information from the interview with material from the detailed Brennglass family tree compiled by Rebecca Weiss and posted on Ancestry.com. See https://www.ancestry.com/family-tree/person/tree/102651872/person/340028198687/facts.

38. Interview with Alan C. Brennglass.

39. Interview with Alan C. Brennglass.

40. Weissbach, *Jewish Life*, concludes on page 118: "America's smaller Jewish communities in their classic era [1880s–1930s] were overwhelmingly composed of entrepreneurs working in retail trade or in commercial ventures such as livestock sales or junk collecting together with their families and white-collar employees. Thus, nearly all small-town Jewish families were part of a broadly defined middle class, or very near its edges."

41. Michael Brown, quoted in Joshua D. Macfadyen, "Nip the Noxious Growth in the Bud": Ortenberg v. Plamondon and the Roots of Canadian Anti-Hate Activism," *Canadian Jewish Studies / Études juives canadiennes* 12 (2004): 74.

42. David Rome, ed., *The Plamondon Case and S. W. Jacobs* (Montreal: National Archives, Canadian Jewish Congress, 1982), 2 vols.

43. Jacques Langlais and David Rome, *Jews & French Quebecers: Two Hun-*

dred Years of Shared History, trans. Barbara Young (Waterloo, Ontario: Wilfrid Laurier University Press, 1991), loc. 1862.

44. David Fraser, "The Blood Libel in North America: Jews, Law, and Citizenship in the Early 20th Century," *Law & Literature* 28/1 (2016): 37.

45. Quoted in Fraser, "Blood Libel in North America," 40.

46. Fraser, "Blood Libel in North America," 40; Macfadyen, "Nip the Noxious Growth," 77.

47. Macfadyen, "Nip the Noxious Growth," 78.

48. Macfadyen, "Nip the Noxious Growth," 78.

49. For the narrative of the trial, see Macfadyen, "Nip the Noxious Growth"; Fraser, "Blood Libel in North America"; and Rome, *The Plamondon Case and S. W. Jacobs*.

50. Quoted in Fraser, "Blood Libel in North America," 53.

51. Quoted in Fraser, "Blood Libel in North America," 43.

52. Fraser, "Blood Libel in North America," 57.

53. Quoted in Langlais and Rome, *Jews & French Quebecers*, 66–67.

54. Fraser, "Blood Libel in North America," 62.

55. Fraser, "Blood Libel in North America," 63.

56. *Le Miroir*, January 3, 1932.

57. Fraser, "Blood Libel in North America," 64.

Chapter 4: The Massena Case and American Antisemitism

1. Interview with Doris Robinson, Massena, New York, June 1, 2015.

2. Interview with Alice Rosen, Masonic Home, Utica, New York, May 31, 2015.

3. Shirley Reva Vernick, *The Blood Lie* (El Paso: Cinco Puntos Press, 2011).

4. Interview with Alan C. Brennglass, New Rochelle, New York, June 8, 2015.

5. Hasia Diner, *The Jews of the United States 1654–2000* (Berkeley: University of California Press, 2004), 43; Paul Johnson, *A History of the Jews* (London: Weidenfeld & Nicolson: 2001), 366.

6. Lindemann, *Jew Accused*.

7. Diner, *Jews of the United States 1654–2000*, 55.

8. Quoted in Diner, *Jews of the United States 1654–2000*, 57.

9. Michael Meyer, *Response to Modernity: A History of Reform Judaism* (New York: Oxford University Press, 1988); Lindemann, *Jew Accused*, 202.

10. Steven R. Weisman, *The Chosen Wars: How Judaism Became an American Religion* (New York: Simon & Schuster, 2018). This argument about America as the new Zion threads through Weisman's entire book. See especially the Introduction and chs. 6, 11, and 13.

11. Weisman, *Chosen Wars*, 53.
12. On Dispensationalism and its relationship to Jews and Israel, see Timothy P. Weber, *On the Road to Armageddon: How Evangelicals Became Israel's Best Friend* (Grand Rapids, MI: Baker Academic, 2004).
13. Weber, *On the Road to Armageddon*, loc. 241–66.
14. Leonard Dinnerstein, *Anti-Semitism in America* (New York: Oxford University Press, 1994), 19.
15. Dinnerstein, *Anti-Semitism in America*, 22.
16. Nathan C. Belth, *A Promise to Keep: A Narrative of the American Encounter with Anti-Semitism* (New York: Times Books, 1979), 17–19.
17. Dinnerstein, *Anti-Semitism in America*, 32–34.
18. John Higham, *Send These to Me: Jews and Other Immigrants in Urban America* (New York: Atheneum, 1975), 121. For a detailed, erudite discussion of Christianity's foundational antipathy to Jews and Judaism, see Nirenberg, *Anti-Judaism*, chs. 2–3.
19. Quoted in Higham, *Send These to Me*, 120.
20. See Zebulon B. Vance, *The Scattered Nation*, many editions, full text at https://archive.org/stream/zebulonbvancethe00maur/zebulonbvance the00maur_djvu.txt.
21. Higham, *Send These to Me*, 126.
22. "Antisemitism in Populist History," http://jewishcurrents.org/tag/william-jennings-bryan/.
23. Quoted in Dinnerstein, *Anti-Semitism in America*, 50.
24. Quoted in Higham, *Send These to Me*, 124.
25. Lawrence Goodwin, *The Populist Moment: A Short History of the Agrarian Revolt in America* (New York: Oxford University Press, 1978).
26. Quoted in Dinnerstein, *Anti-Semitism in America*, 56–57.
27. Dinnerstein, *Anti-Semitism in America*, 59.
28. Dinnerstein, *Anti-Semitism in America*, 62–63.
29. Higham, *Send These to Me*, 130. On lynching, see Painter, "Who Was Lynched?": 577; Pfeifer, *Rough Justice*.
30. Joellyn Zollman, "Jewish Immigration to America: Three Waves," at https://www.myjewishlearning.com/article/jewish-immigration-to -america-three-waves/; Elijah Alperin and Jeanne Batalova, "European Immigrants in the United States," Migration Policy Institute, August 1, 2018, at https://www.migrationpolicy.org/article/european-immigrants-united-states.
31. Zollman, "Jewish Immigration to America: Three Waves"; Alperin and Batalova, "European Immigrants in the United States," 146.

32. Alexis de Tocqueville, *The Old Regime and the French Revolution* (New York: Anchor, 1983 [1856]), Part Two, chs. 8–9.
33. Higham, *Send These to Me*, 148.
34. Higham, *Send These to Me*, 149.
35. Higham, *Send These to Me*, 149.
36. Higham, *Send These to Me*, 153.
37. Higham, *Send These to Me*, 153–54.
38. Higham, *Send These to Me*, 163–64.
39. Quoted in David J. Goldberg, *Discontented America: The United States in the 1920s* (Baltimore: Johns Hopkins University Press, 1999), 24–25.
40. Goldberg, *Discontented America*, 24–44.
41. Jan Voogd, *Race Riots and Resistance: The Red Summer of 1919* (New York: Peter Lang, 2008); Alfred L. Brophy, *Reconstructing the Dreamland: The Tulsa Riot of 1921—Race, Reparations, and Reconciliation* (New York: Oxford University Press, 2003).
42. Goldberg, *Discontented America*, 117–18; Pegram, *One Hundred Percent American*, 7–9.
43. Melvyn Stokes, *D.W. Griffith's The Birth of a Nation* (New York: Oxford University Press, 2007), 3–9.
44. Pegram, *One Hundred Percent American*, 16, 26.
45. Pegram, *One Hundred Percent American*, 43.
46. Pegram, *One Hundred Percent American*, 59–61.
47. Pegram, *One Hundred Percent American*, 66–67.
48. Pegram, *One Hundred Percent American*, 186–91; Goldberg, *Discontented America*, 120.
49. Goldberg, *Discontented America*, 120–24.
50. Quoted in Pegram, *One Hundred Percent American*, 75–76.
51. Quoted in Pegram, *One Hundred Percent American*, 87.
52. Steve Oney, *And the Dead Shall Rise: The Murder of Mary Phagan and the Lynching of Leo Frank* (New York: Vintage, 2004).
53. Quoted in Lindemann, *Jew Accused*, 272. Lindemann downplays the role of antisemitism in this case, but his argument does not convince.
54. Mary Beth Norton, *In the Devil's Snare: The Salem Witchcraft Crisis of 1692* (New York: Vintage, 2002); Emerson W. Baker, *A Storm of Witchcraft: The Salem Trial and the American Experience* (New York: Oxford University Press, 2014).
55. Quoted in Jill Lepore, *New York Burning: Liberty, Slavery, and Conspiracy in Eighteenth-Century Manhattan* (New York: Vintage Books, 2006), loc. 4009.

56. Lepore, *New York Burning*, loc. 82.

57. Angela Y. Davis, *Women, Race & Class* (New York: Random House, 1981), 185–90.

58. Davis, *Women, Race & Class*, 188.

59. Quoted in Pegram, *One Hundred Percent American*, 55.

60. Goldberg, *Discontented America*, 125; Pegram, *One Hundred Percent American*, 54.

61. Quoted in Gordon, *Second Coming of the KKK*, 50. Tom Rice, "How the Ku Klux Klan Used Cinema to Become a Force in America," *New Republic*, December 11, 2015.

62. Rice, "How the Ku Klux Klan Used Cinema."

63. Gordon, *Second Coming of the KKK*, 50–51.

64. For the Catholic population, see Theodore Caplow, Louis Hicks, and Ben J. Wattenberg, *The First Measured Century: An Illustrated Guide to Trends in America, 1900-2000* (Washington, D.C.: American Enterprise Institute Press, 2001), 111. For the Jewish population, see Jewish Virtual Library, "Vital Statistics: Jewish Population in the United States, Nationally (1654–present), at http://www.jewishvirtuallibrary.org/jewish-population-in-the-united-states-nationally.

65. Silver, *Louis Marshall and the Rise of Jewish Ethnicity in America*, 471–73.

66. On the decline of the Klan, see Pegram, *One Hundred Percent American*, chs. 6–7.

67. Steven Watts, *The People's Tycoon: Henry Ford and the American Century* (New York: Penguin Random House, 2005), prologue.

68. Watts, *People's Tycoon*, 378.

69. *New York Times*, April 9, 1935.

70. Watts, *People's Tycoon*, 382–83.

71. Anonymous, *The International Jew: The World's Foremost Problem* (November 1920), loc. 19, 32, 34, 35, 92. This is a compilation of articles published in the *Dearborn Independent* in 1920. The text was republished online by the American Nazi Party, listing the authors as "Henry Ford and the editors of the *Dearborn Independent*" (Aaargh Internet edition, 2003).

72. Anonymous, *The International Jew*, 128–32 (loc. 1814-64). On Ford's denunciation of "Jewish jazz," see Claudia Roth Pierpont, "Jazzbo," *The New Yorker*, January 10, 2005.

73. Neil Baldwin, *Henry Ford and the Jews: The Mass Production of Hate* (New York: Public Affairs, 2001), 222–23.

74. Anonymous, *International Jew*, 14ff.

75. Anonymous, *International Jew*, 36.

76. Anonymous, *International Jew*, 42.

77. Watts, *People's Tycoon*, 379.
78. Silver, *Louis Marshall and the Rise of Jewish Ethnicity in America*, 386.
79. Watts, *People's Tycoon*, 380.
80. Silver, *Louis Marshall and the Rise of Jewish Ethnicity in America*, 391–95.
81. Watts, *People's Tycoon*, 391–92.
82. Watts, *People's Tycoon*, 376, 394.
83. Silver, *Louis Marshall and the Rise of Jewish Ethnicity in America*, 399.
84. Quoted in Silver, *Louis Marshall and the Rise of Jewish Ethnicity in America*, 400.

Chapter 5: The Election of 1928

1. Michaud, *Yesterday in Massena*, 26.
2. On Hoover, see Joan Hoff Wilson, *Herbert Hoover: Forgotten Progressive* (New York: Waveland Press, 1992).
3. Alan J. Lichtman, *Prejudice and the Old Politics: The Presidential Election of 1928* (Chapel Hill: University of North Carolina Press, 1979), 10.
4. Robert A. Slayton, *Empire Statesman: The Rise and Redemption of Al Smith* (New York: Free Press, 2001), 3.
5. Quoted in Lichtman, *Prejudice and the Old Politics*, 10.
6. Lichtman, *Prejudice and the Old Politics*, 11.
7. Robert Caro, *The Power Broker: Robert Moses and the Fall of New York* (New York: Alfred A. Knopf, 1974).
8. Lichtman, *Prejudice and the Old Politics*, chs. 3–6.
9. Charles C. Marshall, "An Open Letter to the Honorable Alfred E. Smith," *Atlantic Monthly*, April 1927.
10. Slayton, *Empire Statesman*, 303.
11. Slayton, *Empire Statesman*, 303.
12. Slayton, *Empire Statesman*, 304.
13. Slayton, *Empire Statesman*, 304–5.
14. Slayton, *Empire Statesman*, xi.
15. Slayton, *Empire Statesman*, 300.
16. Slayton, *Empire Statesman*, 310–11.
17. Slayton, *Empire Statesman*, 64–67.
18. Slayton, *Empire Statesman*, 305.
19. Slayton, *Empire Statesman*, 53.
20. Both quotes from Slayton, *Empire Statesman*, ix–x.
21. Slayton, *Empire Statesman*, 313–14.
22. Pegram, *One Hundred Percent American*, 217–19.

23. The last two quotes from Lichtman, *Prejudice and the Old Politics*, 59.
24. Slayton, *Empire Statesman*, 311.
25. Slayton, *Empire Statesman*, 301.
26. Michaud, *Yesterday in Massena*, 27; *Massena Observer*, March 1, 1928.
27. Ogdensburg *Republican-Journal*, September 8, 1928.
28. *Northern Tribune*, September 5, 1928.
29. *Gouverneur Free Press*, September 21, 1928, and October 26, 1928.
30. Dobbie, Greenblatt, and Levine, *Before Us*, 166.
31. Slayton, *Empire Statesman*, x.
32. Slayton, *Empire Statesman*, 305.
33. Slayton, *Empire Statesman*, 316.
34. Slayton, *Empire Statesman*, 316.
35. Slayton, *Empire Statesman*, 285–87.
36. Slayton, *Empire Statesman*, 289–90, 325.
37. In 1918, Smith won just two counties outside metropolitan New York City. He won not a single non–New York metropolitan county in 1920, nine in 1922, one in 1924, and three in 1928. *Massena Observer*, October 18, 1928. New York State has 62 counties.
38. *Massena Observer*, October 18, 1928.
39. *Massena Observer*, October 25, 1928; Fifteenth Census of the United States: 1930. *Population*, vol. 3, 276. The 1930 census showed 3,645 native-born Massena residents age twenty or older. Since the census divided the younger population into age tranches of four years, twenty through twenty-four and twenty-five through twenty-nine, we have to estimate the number of twenty-year-olds—about 100–150—and subtract that number from 3,645. Doing so gives us 3,500 to 3,550 native-born adults age twenty-one or older.
40. *Massena Observer*, March 25, 1986.
41. *Massena Observer*, September 20, 1928.
42. *Massena Observer*, October 24, 1928.
43. *Massena Observer*, September 20, 1928.
44. *Courier & Freeman*, September 26, 1928.
45. *Herald-Recorder*, November 2, 1928.
46. Canton *Commercial Advertiser*, October 9 and 23, 1928.
47. Canton *Commercial Advertiser*, October 24, 1928.
48. See the ad with this slogan in the *Massena Observer*, September 20, 1928. The Great Depression had little to do with the outcome of the 1928 election. The best economic historians currently maintain that the Federal Reserve's misguided interest-rate hikes in 1928—in the context

of the international gold standard—are what sparked the economic collapse of the following year. See Barry Eichengreen, *Golden Fetters: The Gold Standard and the Great Depression, 1919–39* (New York: Oxford University Press, 1994).

49. *Ogdensburg Advance and St. Lawrence County Sunday Democrat*, October 14, 1928.

50. *Ogdensburg Advance and St. Lawrence County Sunday Democrat*, November 4, 1928.

51. *Ogdensburg Advance and St. Lawrence County Sunday Democrat*, November 4, 1928.

52. *Rochester Catholic*, October 27, 1928.

53. *Gouverneur Free Press*, October 5, 1928.

54. Odgensburg *Republican-Journal*, November 6, 1928.

55. David C. Clark, "Radio in Presidential Campaigns: The Early Years (1924–1932)," *Journal of Broadcasting* VI/3 (Summer 1962): 232.

56. Clark, "Radio in Presidential Campaigns," 233.

57. Clark, "Radio in Presidential Campaigns," 235.

58. Clark, "Radio in Presidential Campaigns," 235.

59. Lichtman, *Prejudice and the Old Politics*, 76.

60. *Ogdensburg Advance and St. Lawrence County Sunday Democrat*, November 4, 1928.

61. Ogdensburg *Republican-Journal*, November 1, 1928.

Chapter 6: A National Affair

1. Boris Smolar, "Incident at Massena Leaves Mark on History," *Jewish News*, December 15, 1978: 21.

2. Smolar, "Incident at Massena Leaves Mark on History," 21; Shulkin to Wise, October 1, 1928, in SWP. "A representative of the J.T.A. [Jewish Telegraph Agency, i.e., Smolar] was here Friday night and Saturday morning. A telegram from Jacob Landau of the Agency explained that the gentleman was coming at the suggestion of Mr. Louis Marshall." In 1928, there were no scheduled trains that would have enabled Smolar to leave New York City late Saturday night and arrive in Massena the following day.

3. Richard G. Richards [Wise's secretary] to Shulkin, September 29, 1928, Western Union telegram in SWP.

4. Silver, *Louis Marshall and the Rise of Jewish Ethnicity in America*, xii.

5. Silver, *Louis Marshall and the Rise of Jewish Ethnicity in America*, xii, and part II, passim.

6. Silver, *Louis Marshall and the Rise of Jewish Ethnicity in America*, 258.
7. Quoted in James Rudin, *Pillar of Fire: A Biography of Rabbi Stephen S. Wise* (Lubbock: Texas Tech University Press, 2015), 179.
8. Rudin, *Pillar of Fire*, 274.
9. All the local papers gave essentially the same story of Barbara's ordeal and happy reunion with her family. See *Watertown Times*, Syracuse *Post-Standard*, Ogdensburg *Republican-Journal* for the week of September 24, 1928.
10. Shulkin to Wise, September 25, 1928, in SWP.
11. *Massena Observer*, October 11, 1928.
12. Interview with Barbara Griffiths Klemens, Hermon, New York, October 27, 2018.
13. Shulkin to Wise, September 25, 1928, in SWP. Italics added.
14. Richards to Shulkin, September 29, 1928, in SWP.
15. Wise to Shulkin, September 29, 1928, in SWP.
16. Wise to Warner, September 29, 1928; Wise to Hawes, September 29, 1928, in SWP.
17. Wise to Dearest Children, October 3, 1928, in SWP.
18. *New York Times*, October 3, 1928. The Marshall letter that appeared in the *Times* was virtually identical to the one he wrote to Major Warner, dated October 1, 1928, in LMP.
19. Smith to Wise, October 3, 1925, in SWP; *New York Times*, October 4, 1928.
20. The text of the statement Wise dictated is in SWP.
21. Hawes to Wise, October 2, 1928, in SWP.
22. Shulkin to Wise, October 1, 1928, in SWP. "The Mayor and trooper asked that we have a conference with them at 2:00 o'clock, Tuesday afternoon [September 25]. We met at the synagogue. The officers came with an attorney. They offered their apology for the act. We informed them that the matter had been referred to a higher authority and we could not accept the apology."
23. Rudin, *Pillar of Fire*, 276.
24. Wise to Dearest Children, October 5, 1928, in SWP.
25. Hawes to Wise, October 4, 1928, in SWP.
26. Wise to Dearest Children, October 5, 1928, in SWP.
27. Quoted in Slayton, *Empire Statesman*, xiv.
28. Marshall to Hawes, October 6, 1928, in LMP.
29. Marshall to Shulkin, October 6, 1928, in LMP.
30. Shulkin to Marshall, October 9, 1928, in LMP.

31. Brennglass to Marshall, October 18, 1928, in LMP.
32. Brennglass to Marshall, October 18, 1928, in LMP.
33. For Hawes's childhood residence, see *Turners Hudson River Directory for 1904–1905* (Yonkers, NY: W.L. Richmond, 1905). For the history of the Jewish community of Tarrytown, a suburb north of New York City on the Hudson River, see Temple Beth Abraham, "Our History," at http://tba-ny.org/about-tba/history/.
34. Frank to Marshall, October 11, 1928, in LMP.
35. *Gouverneur Free Press*, October 5, 1928.
36. Kingston *Daily Freeman*, October 6, 1928.
37. Gastonia *Daily Gazette*, October 16, 1928.
38. See, for example, the *Lebanon (PA) Daily News*, October 8, 1928.
39. *Indiana Evening Gazette*, October 4, 1928.
40. *New York Times*, October 7, 1928.
41. *New York Times*, October 6, 1928.
42. Marshall to Frank, October 18, 1928, in LMP.
43. *New York Times*, October 6, 1928.
44. *Kansas City Jewish Chronicle*, October 18, 1928.
45. *The Modern View*, October 5, 1928.
46. Harry Schneiderman, assistant secretary, AJC, to Marshall, October 30, 1928, in LMP. Letters came in from Galveston, Texas, Patterson, New Jersey, Manchester, Georgia, and Lincoln, Nebraska, among many other places.
47. *Canadian Jewish Review*, October 18, 1928.
48. Diamond to Marshall, October 4, 1928, in LMP.
49. Margulies to Wise, October 8, 1928, in SWP.
50. Clifford to Wise, October 2, 1928, in SWP.
51. Lichtman, *Prejudice and the Old Politics*, 76.
52. *Massena Observer*, November 8, 1928. Hoover beat Smith by 1884 to 1107, and Ottinger defeated Roosevelt 1818 to 1121.
53. Rudin, *Pillar of Fire*, 236.
54. Battle to Wise, October 7, 1928, in SWP.

Epilogue: The Blood Libel in Recent Times

1. *Der Stürmer*, May 1934.
2. Edmund Levin, "The Last Ritual Murder Trial," *Slate*, October 8, 2013.
3. David Engel, "Patterns of Anti-Jewish Violence in Poland, 1944–46," *Yad Vashem Studies* XXVI (1998), 1–39; Jan T. Gross, *Fear. Antisemitism in Poland After Auschwitz: An Essay in Historical Interpretation* (New York: Random House, 2007); Sheryl Silver Ochayon, "Anti-Jewish

Violence in Poland After Liberation," at http://www.yadvashem.org/ yv/en/education/newsletter/33/anti_jewish.asp.

4. I follow here the findings of Ochayon, "Anti-Jewish Violence."
5. Quoted in Ochayon, "Anti-Jewish Violence."
6. Quoted in Ochayon, "Anti-Jewish Violence."
7. Bożena Szaynok, "Antisemitism in Postwar Polish-Jewish Relations," in Robert Blobaum, *Antisemitism and Its Opponents in Modern Poland* (Ithaca: Cornell University Press, 2005), 272.
8. Quoted in Ochayon, "Anti-Jewish Violence."
9. Elissa Bemporad, "Empowerment, Defiance, and Demise: Jews and the Blood Libel Specter under Stalinism," *Jewish History* 26 (2012): 348–54.
10. Bemporad, "Empowerment, Defiance, and Demise," 355.
11. Quoted in Bemporad, "Empowerment, Defiance, and Demise," 356.
12. Bemporad, "Empowerment, Defiance, and Demise," 356–57.
13. Bemporad, "Empowerment, Defiance, and Demise," 358.
14. *New York Times*, February 5, 2005.
15. Bemporad, "Empowerment, Defiance, and Demise," 342.
16. *Telegraph*, London, November 28, 2017.
17. Loriga, "Une vieille affaire," 147.
18. Loriga, "Une vieille affaire," 147–48.
19. *Guardian*, May 22, 2003.
20. *Pasque di sangue. Ebrei d'Europa e omicidi rituali* (Bologna: Società editrice il Mulino, 2007); Loriga, "Une vieille affaire," examines the reaction to this book.
21. Quoted in Loriga, "Une vieille affaire," 149–50.
22. See, for example, Elliot Horowitz, "'The Vengeance of the Jews Was Stronger Than Their Avarice': Modern Historians and the Persian Conquest of Jerusalem in 614," *Jewish Social Studies* 4/2 (1998): 1–39; Horowitz, *Reckless Rites: Purim and the Legacy of Jewish Violence* (Princeton: Princeton University Press, 2006).
23. Yuval, *Two Nations in Your Womb*, ch. 4.
24. Yuval, "Vengeance and Damnation, Blood and Defamation." For the reactions, see *Zion* LIX, 169–414. Each article is prefaced with a long summary in English.
25. Johnson, *Blood Libel*, 112–13.
26. Loriga, "Une vieille affaire," 152ff. See also Johnson, *Blood Libel*, ch. 4, for an excellent commentary on the Ariel Toaff affair.
27. Loriga, "Une vieille affaire," 154.
28. Benny Morris, *The Birth of the Palestinian Refugee Problem Revisited* (New York: Cambridge University Press, 2003, originally published 1988).

Morris has, in recent years, recanted his position. See also Simha Fla-pan, *The Birth of Israel: Myths and Realities* (New York: Pantheon, 1987); Efraim Karsh, *Fabricating Israeli History: The "New Historians"* (London: Frank Cass, 2000); Ilan Greilsammer, *Le sionnisme* ("Que sais-je?") (Paris: Presses universitaires de France, 2005); Greilsammer, *La nouvelle histoire d'Israël: Essai sur une identité nationale* (Paris: Gallimard, 1998). Johnson, *Blood Libel*, ch. 3, writes compellingly about the politics of history writing in Israel.

29. Loriga, "Une vieille affaire," 159n57.
30. Jewish Virtual Library, Encyclopedia Judaica: Blood Libel, at http://www.jewishvirtuallibrary.org/blood-libel.
31. *Jerusalem Post*, August 3, 2015.
32. *New York Jewish Week*, November 30, 2015.
33. Mehdi Khalaji, "The Classic Blood Libel Against Jews Goes Mainstream in Iran," *Washington Institute*, April 21, 2015.
34. Friedman, *Incident at Massena*, 78.
35. Interview with Doris Robinson, Massena, New York, June 1, 2015.
36. On the St. Lawrence Seaway, see Jeff Alexander, *Pandora's Locks: The Opening of the Great Lakes–St. Lawrence Seaway* (East Lansing: Michigan State University Press, 2009).
37. Interview with Doris Robinson, Massena, New York, June 1, 2015.
38. Steven S. Cohen and J. Bradford Delong, *Concrete Economics: The Hamilton Approach to Economic Growth and Policy* (Boston: Harvard Business Review Press, 2016).
39. ProPublica, New York State Subsidies Tracker, "Alcoa," at https://projects.propublica.org/subsidies/companies/alcoa-co7084; *New York Times*, November 24, 2015.
40. HomeFacts, "Massena, NY Unemployment Rate Report," at https://www.homefacts.com/unemployment/New-York/St.-Lawrence-County/Massena.html.
41. *New York Times*, September 19, 2018.
42. See, especially, Richard Russo, *Nobody's Fool* (New York: Vintage, 1994) and *Everybody's Fool* (New York: Vintage, 2016).
43. *Massena Observer*, March 25, 1986.
44. Lawrence Bush, "September 22: A Blood Libel in New York State," *Jewish Currents*, September 21, 2014.
45. Interview with Lenore Levine, Massena, New York, whose grandparents had founded one of Massena's leading stores, June 2, 2015. For the median home value, see https://www.zillow.com/massena-ny/home-values/. The median September 2018 home value in New York State

was $284,000, and in the United States overall, $220,000. See https://www.zillow.com/home-values/.

46. DataUSA, "St. Lawrence County, NY," at https://datausa.io/profile/geo/st.-lawrence-county-ny/.

47. https://www.politico.com/2016-election/results/map/president/new-york/.

48. Vernick, *The Blood Lie*.

Illustration Credits

Index

31192021754005